Warehouse Productivity

Improving Workforce Performance With Simplified Gainsharing

by Pat Kelley & Ron Hounsell, CIRM

Published by the Distribution Group
28 West 25th Street — 8th Floor
New York, NY 10010
(212) 228-0246
www.DistributionGroup.com

ISBN 0915910551
Library of Congress Catalog Card Number: 2005921934

Contents

Appendices

About the Authors

Pat Kelley is the Director of Logistics for True Value Hardware, the corporate umbrella for three hardware co-ops: True Value, Servistar, and Coast to Coast Hardware.

He has been with True Value for 27 years, holding nearly every position in the Logistics organization. In the early 1990s, he ran True Value's Human Resources corporate department for four years, before returning to Logistics. Currently he has seven DCs reporting directly to him, with dotted line responsibility for the other six DCs in True Value's network.

Mr. Kelley is also a widely published author of serious literature, with over 1700 of his writings appearing in journals worldwide. He can be found in the periodicals of Georgia State University, Slippery Rock University, the Air Force Academy, the University of Kentucky, and Kent State University, to name a few. A three-time Pushcart Prize nominee, he has published two paperbacks and is the recipient of the Nassau Review Poetry Award for 2001. Mr. Kelley is currently pursuing his MA.

Ron Hounsell is Director of Logistics Services at Denver-based Cadre Technologies, a leading innovator of fulfillment systems used by logistics service providers, distributors, and manufacturers. He works closely with other Cadre team members, providing a variety of analytical and project management services to assist clients in implementing and improving distribution operations.

He came to Cadre in 2004 from a position as Vice President of Business Development and Marketing with Tom Zosel Associates, a management consulting firm serving the specialized needs of consumer products manufacturers, distributors, and retailers across the United States.

Mr. Hounsell has also held positions with the City of Chicago; McDougal, Littell & Co., a privately held publishing firm where he was Director of Distribution; the Chicago office of Grant Thornton LLP, where he served as Manager, Supply Chain Consulting; and Heyman Corporation, an industry-leading privately held manufacturer and distributor of branded children's apparel, where he was Director of Logistics and Distribution.

He is active in the Council of Supply Chain Management Professionals' (formerly Council of Logistics Management) Chicago Roundtable, APICS, and WERC. He has also spoken at a wide variety of industry and professional meetings and conferences around the country. He has been published in numerous trade journals and magazines on subjects ranging from technology selection and implementation to material handling, operations, productivity improvement, and labor management.

Mr. Hounsell received his undergraduate training at the University of Wisconsin, Madison and his graduate training at Northwestern University. He is also certified by APICS in Integrated Resource Management (CIRM).

Acknowledgements

Pat Kelley would like to acknowledge all the people on whom he afflicted these theories over the years, and who thus helped him greatly: Denny Bratkovich, Gene Brickhouse, Dan Burns, Pete Cahill, Dave Cassesse, Paul Clark, Roy Cooper, Dan Cotter, Bryon Crosby, Bob Cunningham, Jim DeAngelo, Andy DeYoung, Randy Dunn, Paul Farber, Joe Forster, Lonnie Franklin, Steve Frantz, Don Fuller, Gerry Gainer, Tim George, Mike Haining, Phil Hammonds, Roger Hansen, Dave Hatton, Olga Heffner, Fred Herres, Dan Hill, Bill Kasper, Wanda Kelley, Joe Kelly, Jo Larson, Walter Lewis, Bill Livingston, Fred Lobo, Bev McCullough, Diane Nauer, Mike Nichols, Bob Nolawski, Ken Prater, Wendell Provost, Sam Robertson, Mike Rosen, Ed Sankowski, Harry Schaeffer, Tim Schlehuber, John Semkus, Tom Statham, and Carol Steele.

Ron Hounsell would like to acknowledge: Eleanor E. Bernard (writer, friend, and role model), Thomas Willis (writer and mentor), Tom Zosel (a truly creative "industrial engineer"), Alfred L. MacDougal III (leader and enabler) and Rama Ramaswami (editor and friend).

The authors would like to jointly acknowledge the contributions of: The Council of Supply Chain Management Professionals (formerly the Council of Logistics Management) and its Chicago Roundtable, Warehousing Education and Research Council (WERC), Distribution Business Management Association, Tom Zosel Associates, and in particular the True Value Company.

Preface

What is this book all about? We'll show you how to improve — even double — warehouse productivity through workforce resurrection. Forgive the somewhat flamboyant term, but we needed a visionary idea and workforce resurrection precisely targets the principles we want to discuss in this book. Many of these core ideas have been in vogue for quite a few years now — such as gainsharing — while other concepts like goal setting on steroids (shooting for the stars while hoping to hit the moon) have been an intuitive part of managerial practices ever since the first Sumerian businessman logged an oxen sale on a cuneiform tablet.

Yet many businesses flounder or fail with their blue-collar incentive plans, while managerial goal setting goes through two or three iterations each decade (a current example is "Good to Great") with an equal amount of buzz words. If all this is indeed true, what then does *Warehouse Productivity* bring to the table? What new techniques or notes do we add to the cacophony of business advice available on the market today?

The brand new material in *Warehouse Productivity* deals primarily with the refinement of those plans mentioned above. We'll demonstrate how to create a surefire successful implementation. The difference between mediocrity and great success often lies in the details. The goal of this book is to demonstrate methods that will enable your company to see where productivity levels can go if the right formulas, processes and strategies are put into place. Why have a handful of companies hit grand slams with gainsharing or profit sharing, while most companies attempt these innovative programs with much fanfare only to quietly abandon them later? Why do some managerial teams set and hit goals of 30% or 40% increases in productivity, while most companies start their goal setting each new fiscal year by looking first at the inflation rate from the prior year?

We'll provide simple answers to these questions and easy techniques to make the execution of pay-for-performance and goal setting plans significantly more successful. *Warehouse Productivity* illustrates the refinements of these plans, along with some unique twists in application, while also pointing out the pitfalls and landmines. Properly applied, the principles in this book will demonstrate that any workforce can readily resurrect and come alive with profitability.

When you put it all together, the system we're about to describe overcomes the latent tendencies of many business people while harnessing the self-interest of the workforce. Respectfully we point out: Many managers tend to be mathematicians, and most business plans are constructed primarily with numbers. Not that math is bad — but numbers often fail when trying to measure people's discretionary work decisions and output. The Simplified Gainsharing method described in this book overcomes this and works well because it mimics the free enterprise system itself, where an increase in an individual's work effort is linked directly to an increase in earnings.

Our system provides an unstoppable impetus to create significantly enhanced profits. So where the actual components we're about to describe might appear elementary, it's the impetus and avoidance of managerial pitfalls that we believe are brand new. Many leaders of companies employing blue-collar workforces believe there is not much room left in discretionary productivity; we hope to prove in this book there's tons of room left.

As an aid, we've posted rules throughout the book to encapsulate our principles for either a quick refresher of the book or to help you prepare your own speeches and presentations.

So get ready to take a fresh look at your own workforce — we think there's a lot of new life to be easily injected into it!

Chapter 1
An Introduction to Simplified Gainsharing

Executives and managers live their days in a whirlwind of activity. They fly from meeting to meeting to planning session to brainstorming committee, all the while catching and pitching never-ending voicemails and emails. Before they know it, it's night time and they're in the car heading home, wondering what they actually accomplished — it was a wild, busy day, in which they participated 110%, with several great ideas and bold new directions.

All is well with the corporate world. This is the way it should be for the hard-chargers who live in a different dimension of time where days pass ten times faster than they do for the rest of the mortals on this planet. The point to be made here is simply that the workforce these executives direct lives in an entirely opposite dimension of time from the one they occupy.

Time is the enemy for the non-exempt workforce. Time is what you battle when you're in the blue-collar ranks. When you punch a clock, time is something to get through as painlessly as possible during the long, long workday. The average worker will readily tell you, "Hey, I just want to put in my eight hours, then get out of here."

The work day for the blue-collar workers begins when they arrive at the time clock only a minute or so before it's time to punch in. And so it goes — the start bell announces the first round in the fight between the worker and time. The immediate challenge, after this bell rings, is how to get to the next bell which announces the morning break. How many bathroom visits can you get away with? What's for lunch today? Of course lunch is far, far in the distance, and you'll have plenty of time to think about it. And if lunch is a long time away, the afternoon break bell is nearly inconceivable. What about the end-of-the-shift bell? That's a point in time you'll never make, so why torture yourself thinking about it?

So where the executive has this odd love affair with time (a tease who always slips from the grasp), the blue-collar worker battles it, and develops hundreds of strategies — some quite bizarre — on how to get through the day. Time is not the same for all of us.

A survey of employees at work finds 75% of workers know they could be significantly more effective at work; 50% are doing just enough to get by; and 19% actually say they are actively disengaged. Worker apathy, it has been estimated, costs American business up to $300 billion a year.

On the lists of the most boring jobs in America, along with the usual candidates such as security guards and long-haul semi-drivers, we also find factory workers and warehouse and distribution center workers. At first blush, it might appear odd to find these jobs listed as excruciatingly boring, but if one traces their paths during the workday, it becomes evident how these workers basically go in circles — some small, others wide — most of the day. These folks are all on some form of hamster treadmill. Save them!

Gainsharing

Realizing that most people in the workforce are bored out of their gourds quickly helps you understand why gainsharing or profit sharing programs are attractive to employees. The best of these programs quickly cut through boredom, and begin to resurrect many of the dead ones buried in the workforce. And these programs never fail to attract the attention of those workers who are searching for something to break up the monotony of their endless workdays. They welcome anything that will help them feel more in control of their destiny or that enhances their work quality of life.

PRODUCTIVITY RULE #1

Don't judge your workforce from your own dimension of Time. They're bored silly.

On the other hand, such pay-for-performance programs are not an instant panacea for the management team, mostly because they are complex and require specialized skills on the same order as asking a management team to physically resuscitate real accident victims. Not an easy thing, even though all the desire and urgency in the world is present in facility managers and supervisors.

Before we illustrate the pros and cons, let's first take a look at a quick definition and history of these Sharing plans.

Profit sharing is an incentive-based compensation program to award employees a percentage of the company's profits. Some historians trace profit sharing to the whaling ships of the 17th and 18th centuries where everyone on the whaler shared in the ship's profits; but it can be factually traced back to 1820 when the French National Fire Insurance Company was organized, using profit sharing as an element of its employee compensation. Other French businesses picked it up, and it soon attracted the attention of British economist John Stuart Mill. The English used profit sharing quite extensively during the 19th century, along with other countries such as Germany, Italy, Holland, and the Swiss in 1869 even incorporated it into their postal service, although they abandoned it four years later. In the 20th century, many American companies, such as Procter and Gamble, Eastman Kodak and Sears, have used it to success.

Gainsharing is an incentive plan that pays workers based on improvements in the company's productivity. Its core element is employee participation in management practices, and it can be traced back to Joseph Scanlon, who in 1939 implemented it at Empire Steel and Tin Plate Company, using it effectively to keep the company from going out of business. The success of this employee involvement effort led the United Steel Workers to endorse it in other mills. Other plans using participative methods were developed, such as the Rucker Plan and Improshare, and gainsharing has been widely experimented with throughout American business.

PRODUCTIVITY RULE #2

If you want your workforce to resurrect, you must first give them a compelling reason to rise up.

Some companies have been wildly successful with gainsharing programs; others have spent a lot of time, money and effort designing and implementing gainsharing programs only to see them fizzle within a year or two. But regardless of the ultimate success or failure of the plans, one thing is readily admitted by all companies — their employees initially take a lot of interest in these topics.

Simplified Gainsharing

Simplified Gainsharing incorporates the best parts of gainsharing plans (i.e., making a lot of money for companies and employees) while avoiding their pitfalls and speed bumps. Best of all, it's easy to train supervisors and employees on Simplified Gainsharing techniques, and it's inexpensive to implement. Most times, a Simplified Gainsharing program can be designed and implemented in only a month or two; we have included a generic Simplified Gainsharing plan document in Appendix 1.

But before we start on Simplified Gainsharing, let's first look at the pros and cons of full-blown gainsharing plans.

PROS:

• Can be used to significantly increase productivity and quality

• Improves turnover rates and decreases absenteeism

• Increases employee involvement in company goals

• Improves morale.

CONS:

• The program and formulas are difficult to understand, and require extensive training

• Managers and supervisors struggle with the human resource principles

• Requires employee involvement and team-oriented management styles

• Team training and meetings expend a lot of labor hours

• FLSA (Fair Labor Standards Act) requires gainsharing bonuses to be recalculated into hourly gains for payment of overtime.

Pondering these two lists, it becomes almost evident there's a need for a simplified approach. The advantages to gainsharing are immense: there are great productivity gains and quality improvements to be gathered. On the other hand, the disadvantages have sunk many a gainsharing implementation.

PRODUCTIVITY RULE #3

Don't require the managers of your facilities to be Human Resources gurus. Most of them are much better numbers people or engineers.

The problem can be readily summed up by the following premise: If you take any 20 distribution center or plant managers, you'll find two or three of them to be great leaders of the workforce who keenly understand human nature; at the other end of this spectrum, you'll find two or three managers who go brain dead when presented with incentive plans — they just don't get them. In the middle of this spectrum are managers who basically do a decent job of directing their workforces. But the fact remains that the majority of managers are a lot more comfortable with math and engineering than they are with motivational programs. Give them a conveyor to install and they'll jump right in and start charting it out; give them an incentive program to install, and they'll wonder if upper management has lost their minds.

In the end, it's these managers' natures that govern the success of incentive programs. Given that incentives can be wildly powerful and have the potential to return amazing profits, most incentive programs wander, morph and eventually fail in the hands of all but a few intuitively skillful managers.

Free Money

The accountants in your company live in absolute dread of free money.

Free money is what the accountants think everyone on Earth is trying to figure out how to get, and free money is precisely what, the accountants believe, ill-designed pay for performance plans irredeemably hemorrhage to all employees. "You're giving away free money!" they'll accuse in unison as soon as they suspect that labor gains are not in proportion to the bonuses paid out to the employees. And how many pay-for-performance plans do they judge to be ill-designed? Nearly all of them — all the ones, that is, that they didn't have a hand in designing.

So the place to start in any description of a Simplified Gainsharing plan is to counsel you to pledge that you will have your accountants, comptroller, and CFO all wired into the concept of your pay-for-performance plan and make sure they know how the formulas work. Don't make a move without them. More profit sharing and gainsharing programs have been murdered by people worrying about free money than any other single reason, with the possible exception of complexity problems. Avoid this pitfall of leaving your accountants out of the loop. An easy remedy is to make certain the CFO buys into the financial elements of your intended design, then make sure the CFO assigns an accountant to work on, and bless, the Simplified Gainsharing plan design.

Another prudent step is to have an accountant (or their designate) tabulate all Simplified

Gainsharing results and approve the monthly payouts. The bottom line in this discussion is to make sure you keep the financial people involved and comfortable throughout the Simplified Gainsharing process.

Not that we're concerned about the financial formulas, which are simple, or the financial synergies, which are substantial. We're only concerned that the finance people are kept fully in the loop, and are involved right from the very beginning. As we'll show you in coming chapters, the basic Simplified Gainsharing percentages for sharing productivity dollar gains are two-thirds to the company, and one-third to the employees. These percentages are generally enough to appease any accountant, and also enough of a carrot to resurrect your workforce.

PRODUCTIVITY RULE #4

Avoid all appearances of free money. Make certain your plan is blessed up front by the CFO, and the proper accountants are involved in the process.

But be assured we say all this affectionately — some of our best friends are accountants. Yet we also know the tendencies of corporations to kill off golden geese, and we know if the people holding the axes have a hand in giving birth to the golden goose, there is considerably less chance of that goose getting murdered.

And it goes without saying that you should make certain your Human Resource people are involved. Don't do this without them either.

Many companies will recite the mantra that people are their most important asset, but if you truly believe this, you'll do what it takes to implement incentive programs that allow the employees to pay themselves what they think they're worth. Besides eliminating your employees' boredom problems, you'll also greatly improve your turnover rates. In short, your workforce will resurrect and "top-grade" itself. As time passes, you'll spin off the workers who don't want to participate in Simplified Gainsharing, and you'll end up with a top-flight workforce — one you've created yourself.

Since wages and benefits constitute the majority of expenses on the average distribution center's profit and loss statements, it stands to reason that managers should spend the majority of their time in developing labor efficiencies. Not to mention there are few other investments you can make with such a quick and favorable ROI.

Banshees Are Driven To Be Top Producers

The next component to recognize in the drive for resurrection is the concept of the banshees. These are people who set productivity records with a fury. Banshees are workers compelled to always produce at a screaming pace. Every workforce has some of them, and they stand ready to help your resurrection.

If twenty workers are taken at random from the workforce and their productivity and/or quality analyzed, one or two of them will be seen as superlative employees whose performance numbers considerably surpass all expectations. These people are banshees of productivity and it's part of their mental makeup — in their very chromosomes — to always be at the high end of any performance ranking.

At the opposite end of this spectrum, there are two or three employees who have probably inherited some chromosomes from slugs, because their performance is generally sluggish or outright terrible. We'll call these people zombies (to continue our fondness for metaphysical labels in a world of extreme business math). These individuals will eventually self-destruct in the progressive disciplinary process, but the fact remains that if you take twenty employees, you'll find a couple of zombies: people who consistently perform considerably below standards.

In the middle, between these two ends of the spectrum, are the rest of the twenty: workers who span the two extremes, varying from very good workers to good, average, and below average.

PRODUCTIVITY RULE #5

Don't dilute the power of your banshees. They'll set much higher records if you incentify them as individuals, and not as part of a team incentive.

The great news is you probably have a bunch of banshees right now in your own workforce.

There's another facet to the nature of banshees. When you put a banshee on a team incentive, they perform at the same rate as they have in the past, or perform at the same proportion above the average of the group as they always maintained. So if these employees were, in the past, 15% or 20% above the average, that's where you'll always find them. Put in a team incentive, and consequently see the whole group move 10% higher; then you'll see your banshees hover 15% to 20% percent above the new average.

But teams are not the answer. Teams are good, but there's something worrying the banshees who are on the team incentives, something worming its way into the back of their minds. While they're banshees and will always be around 15% above the average, they're a little upset about the zombies. They see the zombies hanging out in the restrooms a lot longer than everyone else; they see the zombies not putting out much effort for the team; and yet they watch the zombies receive the same bonuses as everyone else on the team. So where the banshees will always be banshees, it riles them a tad, it disquiets them a little bit, to know that part of their exemplary effort is helping zombies receive a bonus check.

Again, banshees will never stop being banshees, but they know it's not exactly fair for them to be busting their humps for the greater good of all the zombies. They don't mind helping the average folks get a bonus; for after all, the average folks are trying real hard, but the zombies appear to be taking advantage of the system.

There's a much better way to create gainshares — much more voluminous gainshares.

Individualized incentives are always more powerful than team incentives.

When the banshees are put on team incentives, they'll out-perform average workers but they'll never run at their full capacity.

As a consequence, the company never discovers the top of the envelope on human performance. The banshees never go full tilt. And some companies never realize the full potential of their workforces.

But if the banshees are allowed to fly free and fly as high as they possibly can, they'll pull the entire workforce to higher levels.

This is one of the core ideas of *Warehouse Productivity*.

It only stands to reason that if the banshees are holding back when they're asked to participate in team incentives, they'll excel when placed on a plan that will pay them greater individual bonuses the better they perform and more they achieve. Banshees will find this perfectly fair. "You mean the more we do, the more we'll get?" You can almost see them nodding their heads at the inspired justice of this idea. "And we're working only for ourselves? Not having to carry the zombies?" What could be more fair? "You mean we can actually get paid what we think we're worth?" Buckle your seat belts!

Of course on the other hand, there will be a few who won't think it's fair — the zombies. They endorse the old system. They like the idea that high performers are earning bonuses for them. They'll say that teamwork is the only way to go. "We're a team! Teamwork is what makes our plant the most productive!"

Don't believe them.

Sliding Scales, No Caps

Enabling the banshees to reach their full potential will pull the whole workforce higher. If a banshee can do 40% above standard, they help accustom the rest of the workers to the idea that 10% above standard is easily achieved.

PRODUCTIVITY RULE #6

Teams are good . . . but individual rewards are much, much more powerful.

This also helps validate your disciplinary process. If you have workers doing 30%, 40%, or 50% above standard, how can employees or the union take a position that 10% below standard is acceptable?

The magic that makes all this work is the concept of sliding scales with no caps. Let's take a look at how it works:

Start with all the jobs in your facility for which individual standards can be measured. Tell the workers that if they average 10% above standard for a month, in the following month you'll add something — say 25 cents to their hourly wage for the next month's worth of pay. This is as simple as it can possibly get.

Continue from there: Tell them if they average 15% above standard for a month, you'll add 50 cents to their hourly rate for the following month. And if they average 20% above standard for a month, you'll add 75 cents to their hourly rate for the following month.

And guess what — it doesn't stop there. There is no cap to this thing! Tell your employees that you encourage them to double their productivity, because the sky is the limit to the bonuses you want to pay out. Of course, quality and safety also need to be considered, but more about them later.

How does this one-third/two-thirds gainshare split work? Let's say your employees are making $10.00 per hour, for the sake of simple math. If they perform 10% above standard, they're worth $11.00 per hour to you. And if your benefits average 30% of labor costs, a 10% productivity gain per hour is really worth $11.30 to the company. So for the $1.30 increase on the first 10% gain, you'll pay the employee 25 cents, and the company profits $1.05. The employee gets 19.2% of the gain, the company 80.8%.

Of course, you don't keep this same overwhelming percentage for the next gainshare level. For 15% above standard you pay 50 cents above the regular wage; the savings is $1.95, and the company makes $1.45 as a result. The employee ends up with 25.6% of the gain, the company 74.4%.

One additional point to appreciate: by using a sliding, or stepped, scale to set these new compensation rates, the increased benefit is paid only when the next full step is attained. All value between the steps accrues to the company at no extra cost. In other words, if an employee is performing at 14% above standard, the company only pays the rate for the 10% level.

Examples

Below is an example of one facility's target payouts on Simplified Gainsharing:

% ABOVE BASE		10%	15%	20%	25%	30%	35%	40%	45%	50%
Gainshare payouts		$.25	$.50	$.75	$1.00	$1.25	$1.50	$1.75	$2.00	$2.25
ZONE	Base									
1	130	143	150	156	163	169	176	182	189	195
2	120	132	138	144	150	156	162	168	174	180
3	115	127	133	138	144	150	156	161	167	173
4	130	143	150	156	163	169	176	182	189	195
5	70	77	81	84	88	91	95	98	102	105
6	250	275	288	300	313	325	338	350	363	375
7	65	72	75	78	82	85	88	91	95	98
8	45	50	52	54	57	59	61	63	66	68
9	15	17	19	21	23	25	27	29	31	33
10	60	66	69	72	75	78	81	84	87	90
11	60	66	69	72	75	78	81	84	87	90
12	35	39	41	43	45	47	49	51	53	55
13	85	94	98	102	107	111	115	119	124	128
14	130	143	150	156	163	169	176	182	189	195

Try to keep it as simple as possible. It should be obvious that it's essential to properly establish the baseline (the minimum acceptable level of performance) rate. Simply start at your baseline and go up in increments from there. Some companies begin at 10% above standard, other companies find value in starting at 5% above standard in order to whet their employees' appetites for earning gainshares. Both ways have been successful.

Below is a summary tabulation of Simplified Gainsharing for an actual month in a sample distribution center:

Operational Area	Paid to Emps	Hours Saved	Dollars Saved
REPLENISHMENT	$760.00	174	$2,976.40
SHIPPING	$1,400.00	316	$5,403.60
RECEIVING	$1,300.00	274	$4,685.40
NIGHT SHIFT	$2,200.00	406	$6,942.60
ORDERFILLING	$2,300.00	536	$9,165.60
OFFICE	$800.00	200	$2,798.00
RETURNS	$50.00	12	$206.20
TOTALS:	$8,810.00	1918	$32,177.80
NET TO COMPANY:	$23,367.80		

Note how $8,810 was paid out to the employees in gainshare wage adjustments, which is 27.4% of the $32,178 total dollars saved. This is well within our one-third/two-thirds parameter. And actually, it's considerably below the 33% some might say is due the employees. More on this later.

Corporate Sponsor

Somebody at the corporate level needs to manage the network's Simplified Gainsharing program, and the higher up in the organization that person is, the better the candidate he or she is for corporate sponsor.

Ideally the facility managers will have a reporting relationship to the corporate sponsor, either directly or via a "dotted line." The design, rollout, and administration of a network Simplified Gainsharing program is a time-consuming duty, and it needs to be done by someone who can give direction to facility managers rather than one of their peers. It would be wonderful if the executive in charge of operations could fulfill the role of corporate sponsor, since the facility managers already have a reporting relationship to this position, but realistically there is not enough time to be found in this position to handle these duties in most companies.

So now what? How do you skin this cat, if it's such a time-consuming responsibility? A few suggestions:

Assign the corporate sponsor duties to an assistant VP or director of operations, and have all the facility managers report to this position on a dotted line. Make certain, though, that the position is not over-burdened with prior duties. Corporate sponsorship can be a full-time job. Plus, devoting a high position to Simplified Gainsharing will send a message to everyone in the company that this is a very important mission.

PRODUCTIVITY RULE #8

Lay a strong foundation under your Simplified Gainsharing program before you start: Establish a zealot as corporate sponsor.

An alternative to the above suggestion is to promote one of the current facility managers into this position at a corporate level. Again all the other facility managers need to have a dotted line relationship to this new position. Select a banshee manager who exhibits all the traits described in Chapter 12, "Managerial Best Practices — Benchmarking Your Own Network". The corporate sponsor needs to be a zealot, one who will not rest until Simplified Gainsharing's gospel is accepted by all.

Why do we stress the reporting relationship? Those of us who have labored out in the field quickly come to understand that with operating people it's all about turf and reporting relationships. Indeed this is one of the main reasons there is a dichotomy between HR and the field. Where operating managers are quick to fulfill their bosses' requirements, they are a tad slothful to jump at the newest HR suggestion. Wise companies understand these nuances, and take care to arrange effective reporting organization charts. After all, there's a lot of money at stake — Simplified Gainsharing can have a super-nova ROI, but it can turn into an abrupt black hole if facility managers see it as toothless.

Thus the need for a strong corporate sponsor, and a clear message of support from the executives. Also the corporate sponsor needs to have a good working relationship with the CFO, for Simplified Gainsharing programs live or die based on the sponsor's grasp of finance and an understanding of the finance department. See Appendix 8 for a list of the ideal traits for a corporate sponsor.

Chapter 2
Wages, Not Bonuses

When blue-collar workers get together with workers from other companies, they frequently end up comparing their jobs. Have you ever wondered what they're talking about?

Are they comparing 401k plans? Are they talking about benefits? Or maybe education reimbursement? Or your vacation plans, or pension plans, or the overall working conditions? Sometimes they talk about a few of these, but most of the time they're talking about just one thing: wages. "Hey Fred, how much do you make per hour again?"

The number one determinant of status for blue-collar workers is their hourly wage. It's how the pecking order of the workers in your town is established, it's the bestowal of bragging rights, and the main way a few workers can lord it over all the other workers. "How much to you make? You make ten bucks an hour? Well, over at ABC Company I make eleven bucks an hour. I don't work for chump change, like some people, you know."

Hourly wages are what make the world go 'round for blue-collar workers. So when you base your bonus programs on hourly payouts, you greatly increase the amount of appeal your incentive programs will have to blue-collar people. Lump sum bonuses just don't have the same appeal or the same punch. Give an employee a $100 bonus check, and he'll take it home where his significant other will grab it and buy a piece of furniture. It will be gone in a flash, with no compelling urge for the employee to try to produce another one. But give an employee a 75-cent raise for a month, and this becomes a meaningful event in his life — this automatically ups his status in your town. Plus, he will work hard to make sure he produces another 75-cent raise for the following month, or maybe he'll even shoot for a dollar an hour raise.

At any rate, employees will jump through hoops to try to hang onto that raise. Don't judge their desires by your own fascination for deferred gratification. Some managers will get excited whenever that 401k statement shows up in the mail, and will sit in an easy chair for an hour to wistfully stare at the statement while daydreaming about the amounts they'll have ten, fifteen, twenty years from now. Your employees are not like this! They want instant gratification. When they do something good, they want you to lay the reward in their hands right away. This is why Simplified Gainsharing works so much more powerfully than traditional gainsharing or profit sharing. Indeed, most traditional plans pay off annually, an event so far in the future in your employees' eyes that there's very little impact to the performance/reward relationship.

The ideal system would be for a worker to hit a productivity level one day and get an hourly raise for the next day. Unfortunately, this approach is not practical. Your choice of a pay-out method should depend on the ease of changing hourly rates in your organization. We recommend tracking achievements monthly, and adjusting the wage for the following month. Some companies can manage one week adjustments, so when employees hit a payout level for one week's performance, they get a raise for the following week. In our view, this is even preferable to monthly payouts, since it takes advantage of the concept: do the performance, get the reward right away.

PRODUCTIVITY RULE #9

Don't judge your workforce by your own fascination for deferred gratification. They want a quick hourly raise.

However, don't think that the "new workforce" is only concerned with wages. The general blue-collar population today has somewhat different values from the past. Yes, they'll brag about their hourly wage rates, but they also put more value than their predecessors on time off, on reward and recognition, on quality of work life and on increased control over their situation (as illustrated in this discussion as the ability to increase their compensation). In the following chapters we will discuss these issues (see the section on Free Time Junkies in Chapter 4, for example).

Measure Everything Individually

Most blue-collar jobs can be measured at the individual worker level, and should never be measured by teams or groups in any incentive plan. Even those jobs that traditionally have been measured by the group or department.

How do you measure these jobs individually? When in doubt, just ask your people.

At first blush this might appear counterintuitive. However, every time we've tried this approach, the blue-collar people in the jobs have unfailingly told us how to measure their own productivity.

For example, one company experienced considerable seasonal business that caused anomalies in the measurement of the shipping docks. Management and the dock supervisor attempted to define an individual measurement, but it stalled because of the anomaly between weight and pieces. If they used a pounds per hour measurement for the loaders, productivity unrealistically blipped upward in the winter when they shipped the spring fertilizer, and conversely, pounds per hour productivity dropped in the fall when the docks shipped artificial Christmas trees.

The opposite happened when they attempted a cartons-per-hour measurement. Bags and pallets of fertilizer killed this metric, while all the little cartons of Christmas ornaments inflated the metric. The managers became stymied!

Finally, they called a meeting of the loaders and laid the problem out in an impromptu brainstorming session. The problem was soon solved when one of the loaders suggested they use both metrics. "How can we use both?" one of the managers asked. The loader responded, "Couldn't you set up the sliding scales on both metrics, then pay gainshares off the performance of the lowest metric? This would keep us pushing for production whether or not we were getting a bounce on one of the metrics."

This solved the problem. During fertilizer season, the loaders pushed to load as many pieces as possible, and during Christmas season they pushed to attain the most pounds per hour. It turned out to be an elegant solution, and even more elegant since the people in the department thought of it themselves. Indeed, we often wondered how the people would have reacted if management had dreamt up this solution — probably not as enthusiastically.

The result of this approach is individual measurements in jobs that have traditionally been measured by team numbers, or not measured at all. Why do blue-collar people have an interest in developing fair (i.e., accurate, objective, and consistent) metrics?

Some blue-collar people will readily buy into the concept of being measured so they can earn gainshares; others truly believe in the concept of a fair day's work for a fair day's pay. But these aren't the main motivators. The main reason — and this might sound a tad jaded — is that the blue-collar people are just like your accountants. They too don't want to see people earn free money. And they don't want people in other sections accusing them of earning free money; so there's a lot of motivation from peer pressure at work here.

It's akin to the banshees not wanting to bust their humps to earn bonuses for zombies. The overriding motivation in all this is that blue-collar people have a basic, and strong, belief in fairness. If they help set a baseline level that's 20% below reality, they know that a bunch of people will be earning free money. And if they are part of the group earning the free money, they know that they themselves will be liable to accusations that they are taking free money.

PRODUCTIVITY RULE #10

When needing help in setting or establishing individual standards, try asking the work groups themselves. Blue-collar workers have a surprisingly deep interest in fairness and accuracy.

Even though it's counterintuitive, and one might be suspicious that blue-collar people might set the baseline lower in order to create easier gainshares, we have not found this to be the case. Supervisors in these studies frequently admit that the numbers they had in mind were actually lower than those the blue-collar people recommended. The test is very simple; since team standards and productivity records exist, the workers' recommendations on how to measure individually should add up to or exceed the historical team records.

Another option to avoiding team measurement is to look at the methods and procedures for those tasks from a best practice perspective. There may very well be justifiable reasons for changing the processes that will also facilitate individual tracking.

Why re-invent the wheel when there are other supervisors in your network dealing with the same problems? One receiving supervisor struggled with attaining a fair unloading sliding scale because he knew a receiver could be on a good month with unloading, only to have it ruined if a number of extremely difficult check-ins showed up in a particular week.

In this distribution center (DC), the receivers were assigned to doors, and had to work whichever trucks the receiving clerk assigned to the door. Under this condition, a receiver's gainshares could be harmed or aided by the degree of difficulty of the assignments. Perplexed, the supervisor called some of the other DCs in the network, and quickly discovered a best practice in a DC which had implemented Simplified Gainsharing a few months earlier: Instead of assigning receivers to doors, this receiving department rotated the easy and difficult unloads, making sure each receiver was given a fair chance at increasing their gainshares. It took a little more supervisory time to do this, and it required a little more trust from the receivers that their supervisor was spreading the work fairly. But in the end, it resulted in a level playing field for all the gainsharers, which always helps increase departmental productivity.

One cautionary note: Some managers feel it's unwise to rely solely on the hourly employees, or any other single source, as the basis for establishing metrics. See Appendices 1 and 2 for a detailed discussion on additional methods of establishing and validating baselines and metrics.

Small Teams

Although we said that you should never measure performance by teams or groups in an incentive plan, there are some jobs that simply cannot be measured individually. In such cases, determine the smallest number of workers that can be measured as a team, then use the basic Simplified Gainsharing formula: achievement for one month, then pay raise for the following month.

PRODUCTIVITY RULE #11

Though not as good as individual measurement and recognition, small teams can work well — but shoot for the smallest number of people per team as possible. The same dynamics of banshees and zombies will quickly develop.

How do you create the smallest teams possible to do Simplified Gainsharing? Easy. Just ask the workers involved. Tell them what you have in mind, and that you want to create the smallest possible teams in order for you to begin a brand new incentive system. They'll tell you how to do it.

Distribution centers actually offer a lot of opportunity, specifically because workers in warehouses or distribution centers are not wedded to machines or production lines. These workers have a lot more discretionary activities woven into their overall productivity rates. For example, orderfillers go to many different bin locations for each order; lift drivers pick up and move freight to and from varying places; shippers and loaders put varying cubes and weights into trucks.

Though most jobs in distribution centers are, as a rule, comparatively easy to measure individually, not all jobs in the DCs fall into this category. For instance, the function of loading a truck might encompass consolidating, counting, and loading, with an overall measurement of pounds per labor hour. The job of shipping one truck might be done by two or even three workers. In this case, the team might be just those two or three workers, but based on the same Simplified Gainsharing principles. If the small team achieves the gainsharing levels, then give them all a raise for the following month.

Here's a tip: When the workers tell you how to define or create the smallest teams possible, and you're about to start Simplified Gainsharing, allow them to be the ones to pick the individuals for their team. This might appear unfair to some workers, since the banshees in the department are going to jump on the same team. And as a result of the self-selection process, you'll see that the zombies will all end up on a team. But this is all good. Even using the small team concept, you need banshees to drive the gains upward.

Measurement Options

In order to do Simplified Gainsharing, you must start with valid measurements.

Working with blue-collar work groups in order to establish the baseline metric for individual measurement has always been relatively easy and effective; however, not all companies are going to be comfortable with this method. There are two other sources for establishing the metric: historical records and engineered standards. Regardless of which method you use, it's essential for any workforce resurrection that your plant or distribution center is measuring productivity and has either implemented standards or clearly understands the averages.

One prerequisite for establishing standards is to be knowledgeable about the historical records. Most workplaces have kept track of production records from the past, and many of the jobs have been tracked per individual workers, so it's relatively easy to establish baselines and orient new employees as to what the minimum expectations are in the work place.

But what do you do if the workplace has never been measured in this way? One place to start is to simply begin tracking all jobs on a per-labor-hour basis, tabulating the number of pieces or lines or volume each individual produces. If you're in a quandary over the best method to use to measure a worker, we recommend you simply ask the work group. They will tell you, to the extent of their knowledge and experience. And whatever method they think is fair is a giant clue on the right measurement to use. Just make sure to have your supervision validate the fairness of the recommended measurement to the company.

All this might sound very well and good, but is there a more structured way to establish metrics? The answer is, "of course." Bring in the industrial engineers. They'll be happy to come in to perform time and motion studies, and in our experience you'll generally be presented with recommended standards at levels that will produce a 15% to 30% gain in productivity. Interestingly this approaches the rule of thumb that says whenever you begin to measure work groups that have not be measured in the past, you generally see a 10% to 15% gain in productivity. Just by measuring! The trick is to sustain those improvements, and that's almost entirely a function of the training accorded to managers and supervisors who will also need to perform in the system, just like the hourly employees.

In the big picture, the difference in approaches lies in having an objective way to determine where the bar should be. "This is how high we've gotten the bar in the past," certainly will be an improvement over "This is where I think it should be," but both will land significantly farther from the full potential of workforce performance than engineered standards, or ELS with incentives. When properly implemented, engineered standards also are less susceptible to union challenges than other means of setting expectations.

The key to success, regardless of the approach chosen, most often lies with the quality of the management and supervisory team.

In our experience, the largest factors in improving performance are establishing the right metric, providing ample training for the work force, and improving management's skill in working in a production-oriented environment, with the latter mattering most.

If you're voting to use industrial engineers, we applaud your decision, although there are a few downsides we want to discuss in the next section.

Engineered Standards

The practice of establishing engineered labor standards (ELS) dates from the early 20th century, and it has been widely used in some industries, especially the grocery trade, for more than 30 years.

There are several helpful definitions of engineered standards. One is that it is an accurate measure of a specific operation or operations to be used by management to communicate with employees objectively about performance and productivity. The standard is a means by which to quantify the time required to perform a unit or units of work, based on defined methods and procedures. A standard provides an accurate means of comparing what was anticipated to what actually happened. Finally, an engineered standard defines a minimum expectation for performance for a given work function.

PRODUCTIVITY RULE #13

ELS is an excellent way to establish minimum expectation, and a great platform to launch Simplified Gainsharing.

Taken from another perspective, a standard defines the minimum level of performance which can be reasonably expected from an average trained worker with normal skills, utilizing proper methods and working at a normal pace, under normal working conditions. It should also be noted that work quality will be as good or better in a standards environment as it is prior to the implementation of standards; often it improves significantly.

Engineered standards are rooted in a scientific tradition of measurement and calculation. Despite this fact, as is the case with any other productivity improvement initiative, there are pitfalls with using standards. Standards also have their own, unique mythology. We'd like to discuss two significant components to the "art" of developing an effective improvement program using engineered standards.

The high degree of variability in facility activities means that there will always be trade-offs between those components of an activity that can be measured precisely and those which cannot. How those are treated in the formulation of a standard may differ from engineer to engineer or from one iteration of a standard to another. That's part of the art. If designed properly, however, every calculation of the standard time associated with a task should be the same, and across a large range of instances of any given standard activity, the formula will represent the time content of the work task with great precision.

The second art element centers on how the process is presented to users and managers, how they are trained, and how well the program is understood and accepted. The single biggest factor in success or failure of an initiative using engineered standards is the same as with gainsharing — the perception held by users, supervisors, and managers. It by far outweighs any technology factors, any complexity issues and any accuracy or timeliness problems. When the process is credible, when it's understood and accepted as helpful rather than constraining, it provides the single most effective tool for managing the labor resource in the warehouse, especially when combined with a highly effective incentive program like Simplified Gainsharing.

PRODUCTIVITY RULE #14

Design a system to equitably gain maximum benefit from the improvement effort. Provide thorough training for supervisors and managers as well as hourly employees.

There's a potential inherent danger that many blue-collar employees may perceive it as science and as such it might put a psychological cap on the potential productivity gains from a particular work area. For example, employees will get to thinking, "If the industrial engineers say 100 per hour is the scientific standard, isn't it beyond the bounds of physics to ever achieve 200 per hour . . . or 175 . . . or even 150? You can't do the scientifically impossible, can you?" On the other hand, when users and managers understand the standard (like a piece rate or a historical average) as the minimum acceptable level of performance (a C on a school spelling test, not an A), performance is not constrained by perception.

There are no boundaries to the potential of human performance; there are no limits to human creativity and the ability to think outside the box, or to achieve solutions that boggle the pedestrian mind. This is all akin to the psychological boundary in everyone's mind in past eras concerning breaking the four minute mile. Don't put a lid on your employees' minds!

There's an easy solution. When you bring in your industrial engineers, don't announce that you're establishing engineered standards. Simply announce that the industrial engineers are here to establish a fair starting point for Simplified Gainsharing. "To keep everything fair and square, we need to know what's fair to the employees while being fair to the company. The industrial engineers are here to show us where the fair starting places are for our sliding scales with no caps."

PRODUCTIVITY RULE #15

Don't put psychological caps on your employees' minds: palatably present the metrics as minimum acceptable levels of performance.

Another nomenclature option is to introduce them to your workforce as "Improvement Managers" instead of "Industrial Engineers." This will enable you to avoid the stigma of science and the possible psychological limitations it can place in your workers' minds.

The whole point here is we need to view engineered standards in a new light — like the un-cola. We need "un-engineered" engineered standards to provide a starting point where workers can launch the resurrection.

Chapter 3
Establishing Quality Qualifiers

For every job where you measure productivity by the individual, you must also have a quality qualifier. You need this qualifier so everyone knows that if they are not conscious of their quality, they'll put their Simplified Gainsharing raises in jeopardy.

Once you establish the sliding scales with no caps, you must establish, at the same time, a quality threshold that workers must hit in order to keep their gainsharing payouts. Without a quality qualifier, a worker could go crazy on productivity and throw all quality concerns to the wind in order to earn the highest possible payouts on Simplified Gainsharing. For example, if your productivity sliding scale starts at 100, even the most average of workers could do 200 if they didn't have to worry about quality. So you need a qualifier to keep everyone quality-conscious. Besides, if productivity is implemented properly, quality will go up!

PRODUCTIVITY RULE #16

Set a quality qualifier so nobody goes crazy/sloppy on productivity. But don't use such a high qualifier that it kills the geese that lay the golden eggs.

Where do you put the quality qualifier? The answer is really quite easy: put it at the same place where you have your disciplinary standard for unacceptable quality.

Why not higher? Why not put it at an exemplary level? The reason is you would be killing the geese that lay the golden eggs. It should be a key, public declaration during your Simplified Gainsharing implementation that you want people to earn payouts. You want a lot of people to earn gainshare raises.

So set the quality qualifier at a low enough level where it doesn't knock any reasonable worker out of achieving a gainshare raise, but not so low that you would create quality problems for yourself. That's why your current disciplinary point for quality is the perfect place to set the qualifier.

If workers don't care about their quality, then they don't deserve a gainshare. That's just fair. But you don't want to set the qualifier at such a high level that you knock a lot of workers out of their gainshares. For instance, imagine you're a worker who hit a 35% level on the productivity sliding scales, only to lose it all due to an overly strict quality qualifier. You would feel duped. "Sure, I bust my hump all month long, and earn the company a 35% increase, then they steal it all back from me."

This is why you set the qualifier at your existing quality disciplinary threshold. Nobody can argue that they should still get a gainshare even though they're so sloppy they fall below the disciplinary standard.

But can you use Simplified Gainsharing to drive your quality levels higher? Yes.

Super Quality

Simplified Gainsharing can also be used to greatly improve the quality of your facility through "super quality gainsharing." But care should be taken to frame your quality incentives in a manner that doesn't deflect your productivity efforts.

First, use the same principles established for productivity on Simplified Gainsharing. Determine which jobs can be measured individually as it relates to quality. Let's use an orderfiller in a distribution center as an example. Clock numbers can be assigned to distinct customer orders, so that if the orders contain mispicks, errors can then be assigned to individual orderfillers. A simple ratio of errors per lines picked can be tabulated on a monthly basis. This is pretty basic stuff, and many DCs use these numbers (along with customer requirements) to develop their quality standards. You can use this ratio to pay gainshares as a monthly hourly raise.

PRODUCTIVITY RULE #17

If you can measure quality by the individual, you can use Simplified Gainsharing to significantly improve your facility's quality.

Second, set the target levels for super quality gainshares at the high end of the spectrum. For example, if your disciplinary minimum for orderfilling quality is one error for every 135 lines picked, and your orderfillers as a group average one mistake for every 200 lines picked, you might want to set your gainshare level at one mistake for every 500 lines picked. This creates a level of excellence that only the best of orderfillers will attain. This is the right place to begin a quality gainshare, because you don't want to set it at a level where the majority of workers think they can readily attain it. You don't want super quality to gut your productivity gainshares.

Have we flipped out? What's wrong with improving everyone's quality?

Nothing's wrong with improving quality, of course, but productivity gains are what drive the financial synergies of Simplified Gainsharing, and your program needs to continue to contribute increased profits to the company if you expect it to be funded into the future. So productivity needs to be the main focus of your program, and it needs to be the main target of those employees who want to earn gainshare hourly raises.

Many companies have difficulty applying real dollar measurements to quality. Staying with our orderfilling example, we could ponder for years the actual cost of a mistake in an order. If the customer exchanges a mispick or re-orders a shortage, what is lost really boils down to initial customer satisfaction, and not really a margin loss. On the other hand, if the customer gets so frustrated by the mistake that they never re-order, the error has been an incredibly costly one.

The point to be made on quality gainshares is: are they cost justified?

While it's not science, one distribution network answered this question by asking their DC managers to subjectively put a pencil to framing the dollar savings earned by an individual's exemplary quality. The question was, "If you can improve an orderfiller's quality 50% (cutting their current error level in half), what is that worth to your DC in dollars for a month?" The average answer from sixteen DC managers was $2,500 per employee per month. Of course, for industries such as pharmaceuticals or electronics, these numbers could be much higher.

By setting the top quality gainshare per month at $1.50 per hour, you'd only be paying each employee a $240 per month raise (in a 160-hour work month).

Super Quality Raises

In the land of super quality, you can use a sliding scale to determine quality gainshare hourly raises, but you can't use a sliding scale with no caps. Quality is not the same measurement as productivity. Where there are no upper limits, theoretically, to productivity, there is an absolute upper limit to quality — perfection. You can't have a sliding scale that goes past perfect!

So there are two basic ways to do quality gainshares for individual workers. One way is to create levels between excellence and perfection and pay twenty-five cent raises at each level for a month of achievement. For example: if your disciplinary standard for orderfilling quality is one error for every 135 lines picked, and your orderfillers as a group average one mistake for every 200 lines picked, you might want to set your gainshare level at one mistake for every 500 lines picked. Converting it to ratios, you would have a disciplinary monthly rate at 0.74%, and a twenty-five cent gainshare at a monthly rate of 0.20%. The next twenty-five cent raise would occur at 0.15%, then at 0.10%, 0.05%, and finally, at 0.00%.

Quality Gainshare Levels: 25 cents	
0.20%	25 cents
0.15%	50 cents
0.10%	75 cents
0.05%	$1.25
0.00%	$1.50

A second way to do this is to identify an exemplary level of individual quality, one projected to be achieved by only a handful of employees. But since it's such a challenging goal or level, change the hourly raise. Using a similar example as the one above, set the one exemplary goal at 0.10% and give the employee a fifty cent raise for a month's achievement at this level. The twist is to pay a full dollar raise if the employee can achieve this for a full two months, and $1.50 if they can attain it for three months. Perhaps cap it at $1.50.

PRODUCTIVITY RULE #18

Use Super Quality gain-share hourly raises to significantly improve quality.

If an employee attains one of these levels, but then turns in a month's performance below the exemplary level, the employee will revert to the next level down. For instance, if an employee meets the threshold in three consecutive months and is earning a $1.50 quality gainshare, but then in the fourth month turns in a rate worse than 0.10%, his quality gainshare would fall to $1.00 per hour. If in the fifth month his quality measurement is better than 0.10%, he would regain the $1.50.

Quality Gainshare Level: .10%	
One month	50 cents
Second consecutive month	$1.00
Third consecutive month	$1.50

We recommend a ceiling on this — since you're giving out 50-cent raises — and think you should cap this program at $1.50 per hour in quality gainshares.

High Productivity Equals High Quality

High productivity equals high quality. The more productivity improves, the better quality grows as a natural consequence. This might be the most counterintuitive principle we put forth, but it's real.

PRODUCTIVITY RULE #19

Here's the formula: high productivity equals high quality. Concentration is the main ingredient of both productivity and quality.

In our long careers, we've continually noticed a distinct relationship between many high-productivity workers and many high-quality workers — they turn out to be the same employees. It appears, at first, to be an anomaly, but the more you look into it, the more of a relationship you discover between high performance in productivity and high levels of quality.

An easy way to prove this counterintuitive theory is to simply pick out the top five productivity performers in a facility, where individual measurements are used, and see if they are indeed among the best performers in quality. It doesn't happen in every case, but it occurs with such regularity that it's uncanny.

Why? Unless a worker throws all caution to the wind in the pursuit of high productivity levels (which would cause a quick burnout in the disciplinary process), the worker must concentrate keenly in order to achieve the upper Simplified Gainsharing production levels. You cannot achieve high productivity unless you throw your whole mind into the endeavor. And it's keen concentration that's the main ingredient of great individual quality; just as the inverse is true — it's lack of concentration (perhaps from boredom?) that's the culprit behind anyone's individual quality problems. Concentration is the key determinant!

Interestingly, you can find this same counterintuitive principle at work when you consider the productivity and quality rankings of whole facilities. So often that it's uncanny, too. The top facility in productivity is often the top facility in quality. The same relationship is found when you go to the bottom of the productivity and quality rankings for a company's facilities. It's all about concentration. And you can find this relationship among individuals, teams, sections and whole facilities.

So when a Simplified Gainsharing plan is installed in a facility, and productivity is accentuated by the establishment of gainshare payout levels, the facility gets a natural lift in quality improvement as many employees concentrate on attaining the productivity levels. Then when the individual quality gainshares are established, the facility reaches even higher levels of quality. It's counterintuitive, but true.

Chapter 4
Plug & Play: Implementing Simplified Gainsharing

What we hoped we've illustrated is a very simple gainsharing plan that is easily understood by everyone: it needs to be equally and readily comprehensible to the plant manager, the supervisors and all the employees. This is the essence of the plan we're proposing. People need to be able to look at it, and get it the first time around. "Okay, let me get this straight — if I hit in at 25% above standard for a month, you'll pay me an additional dollar per hour for every hour I work in the following month."

Right.

We think Simplified Gainsharing is so simple it could be termed a Plug & Play system. Nobody needs to be an HR guru. But more important than the employees readily understanding Simplified Gainsharing, the plant manager and all the supervisors can pick up on it right away. You can just hear them telling the employees: "We encourage everyone to figure out how to hit 50% above standard, because then we can pay at two dollars an hour above your regular rate for the next month."

The importance of the Plug & Play concept — where everyone tunes in fast to the concept — is that it will turn your Simplified Gainsharing program into something sustainable for the next decade or so. More gainsharing plans have crashed and burned due to complexity than anything other single reason. Many failed plans are based on teams or employee involvement or participative management — all great concepts and wonderful in theory. But try explaining to the average manager that you want them to set up a system where the employees are going to be formed into teams, then taught how to make decisions by consensus so they can help the manager run the whole plant. The average manager will have absolutely no idea how to accomplish this oxymoronic chore.

But let's say a company truly wants to travel down the participative path. With the proper amount of training, the average manager can certainly tune into these participative management concepts. The next step is to train all the supervisors. This generally takes a couple of months. And then you're ready to start training the employees on how to make team decisions and read Profit and Loss (P&L) statements. This takes another couple of months, not to mention burning up hundreds and hundreds of production hours while your employees sit in meetings. Help!

But finally, everyone is trained and most will parrot all the buzz words and phrases while all agree that this is a brave new era that is playing out in the plant.

We give it less than a year in the average plant or distribution center.

We're not saying the glass is half-full. We're simply saying that for all the time and training effort put into such plans, the process generally collapses under its own weight. It's just too darn hard and cumbersome to keep the attention of the average participant, whether worker, supervisor or manager. Not to mention that the banshees quickly begin to feel they're being used when they see the zombies earning bonuses.

THE FRONTIER

The blue-collar workforce — it's not the final frontier, but in more than a few executives' minds, it's a major frontier all the same, a giant impediment to their profits.

Many executives feel there's really not much room left for improvements in the discretionary productivity of their blue-collar workforces. In reality, there's a ton of room for improvement; so much, in fact, that most facilities can double their productivity over a five- to seven-year period when using Simplified Gainsharing.

PRODUCTIVITY RULE #21

If blue-collar labor and benefits comprise 60% of your P&L expense, spend an appropriate amount of time each day improving your labor costs.

Many executives are not comfortable discussing the workforce or even considering the views of blue-collar people. They don't empathize with them, nor do they really understand the blue-collar mindset. Many executives feel blue-collar workers are a poorly educated group who live in a totally different world. As a consequence, many executives sidestep discussions on most blue-collar topics, with the possible exception of thinking their jobs would be a heck of a lot easier if there weren't all these blue-collar people clogging up their facilities.

To the uninspired, it's inconvenient to have all these blue-collar employees around, but the fact remains that in many companies the blue-collar payroll makes up one of the largest, if not the very largest, line on the P&L statements. Indeed in some companies, hourly payroll and benefits comprise 50%, 55%, or even as high as 65% to 70% of the entire P&L statement. So wouldn't it make sense to pay a lot more attention to these topics? Absolutely. If blue-collar people make up 60% of our expenses, it's certainly reasonable for facility managers to be spending 60% of their time in improving labor costs. Although this never happens.

The truth of the matter is that American management is not spending an appropriate and proportional amount of time on improving blue-collar performance. It's fair to opine that the majority of managerial time should be spent on drilling down on ways to significantly reduce labor costs. But instead, managerial time is spent on daily maintenance items such as keeping the facility running, whether it's sitting in the purgatory of meetings, or responding to the never-ending customer, employee, union, or headquarters requests. Most managers go home each day thinking they were extremely busy, but also wondering what it was they actually accomplished.

Wouldn't it be a lot more effective for all managers to carve out at least an hour each day to brainstorm — or at least spend quality time — on improving the labor costs?

Now let's get back to executive avoidance of blue-collar topics: This avoidance frequently drops into the "dark side of the force," to stay with sci-fi metaphors. This leads some executives to devalue their blue-collar workforce. Sometimes executives perceive their blue-collar workers as louts who can't think much beyond the next payday. Such discounting is unfortunate.

One consequence of this devaluation of blue-collar workers is the Full Time Equivalent (FTE) disease. What's that? The first sign is when executives start talking about headcounts. "How many full time employees do we have in that facility? If we cut out fifty of them, what will that make our labor ratio?" (The labor ratio for a DC is determined by dollars paid for wages divided by sales. Many DCs will separate labor ratio into different categories: for example, warehouse labor, warehouse labor loaded — including benefits — office labor, and salaried labor.)

If the sole approach to improving blue-collar productivity is the creation of headcut plans, your company is in trouble. The trouble is elementary: when workers realize you're laying them off to try to decrease your labor expenses, they immediately slow down — both consciously and subconsciously — to protect their jobs. The real victim of FTE disease is the company, since excessive overtime is now required to get products out the door.

The better way to do this is to improve your bottom line by increasing productivity with Simplified Gainsharing, then allow attrition (not hiring replacement workers when workers quit) to take effect.

Free Time Junkies

Recall for a few moments, if you will, our remarks concerning the nature of time. Your employees live in a different dimension of time than the one you yourself occupy.

Since there is such a large difference in the way different groups of people experience time at work, it stands to reason that Simplified Gainsharing can be employed to motivate people beyond the realm of financial incentives. For many employees, Free Time is a much greater motivator than the ability to earn extra money. Indeed, if time is the enemy, you might be able to show your employees how to defeat this enemy. Here's how it works:

Let's say an employee's average hourly wage is $10.00, and the employee grosses $400.00

for a forty-hour week. Now let's say this employee puts in a month at the 20% gainshare level, and the next month receives $11.00 per hour due to the gainshare bonus structure. That's clear enough — but there is another way for the employee to take a gainshare.

As employees in your facility zoom off on Simplified Gainsharing, a considerable amount of "extra" labor hours will be generated as a result of improved productivity. In the example quoted above, a 20% increase in this employee's production will result in eight hours a week not needed in this employee's section. Multiply this by all the employees in the facility who are on gainshares, and you will realize a certain amount of loosening-up, or slack, in the labor hours needed to run your facility. Until attrition from turnover removes the superfluous employees from the workforce, you can use a free time system to tighten up the labor usage.

PRODUCTIVITY RULE #22

Help your employees combat boredom. Issue free time.

Free time is the granting of time off to employees after all the work is completed in their section. They are allowed to go home early, unpaid, without it being charged on the attendance policy. As such, it's the perfect antidote to the boredom they fight. And many employees would rather take time off than take the extra money per week.

As an aside: Never force employees to take free time if they want to stay at work. This will backfire on you, as the employees get the idea you are using Simplified Gainsharing to take hours away from them. This could quickly ruin your whole Simplified Gainsharing program. Instead, allow your employees to sign up for free time on a voluntary basis. Many facilities have discovered large groups of employees are thrilled to death to take off from work without getting paid, provided they are not charged on the attendance policy.

In fact, there's a particular type of employee who will take all the free time offered. Some could even be termed "free time junkies"; they are so bored in their work that they become addicted to taking time off whenever possible. Some will take whole days off, even whole weeks off. In one especially well-run facility we know, management asked for ten volunteers to take 30 days of unpaid time off, with paid benefits, during a slow period. They received eighteen applications for the ten spots.

Prudently, there's a way for everyone to win in free time. The employee in the example above, who came in at 20% above standard and now earns $11.00 for the next month — that employee could work only 36.4 hours a week at $11.00 per hour and still take home the same $400 gross. The employee wins in the fight against boredom, and the company wins by shedding unneeded labor hours. In Appendix 4 there's a graphic that can be used to illustrate this idea to your employees.

The Nuances of Free Time

Every human being is passionate about something. If you don't believe this, just go to your office window and observe how your employees exit the facility at the end of shift bell.

You'll see some employees go running out their door, their arms raised in the air as though they had just won an Olympic relay race: We're free! We're free!

The point here is: The very employees who are so bored in your facility that they're walking around like they're the survivors on the *Poseidon Adventure* come alive at the end of the day. They are passionate about their freedom. Consider that desire. As a manager or executive, you have vastly different viewpoints concerning time and finances. There are employees who are not interested in increasing their earnings but are very interested in participating in a sliding scale of free time. Some people turn into banshees of free time. And we've even seen some employees who don't tell their significant others that they're gaining a lot of free time at work; instead they bring home a regular forty-hour paycheck while turning their gainshares into "go'n fish'n" time.

One of the nuances of free time revolves around the question of how it is disseminated throughout the whole facility. Basically there are two ways to do it. One way is to base it on a facility-wide basis, and tell the employees that when every section in the facility is current, then free time will be offered for the remainder of the day. You'll have to decide whether to offer free time on a "first come, first serve" basis, or offer it on a seniority basis.

PRODUCTIVITY RULE #23

Don't judge your employees based on your values related to financial gain. For some employees, free time is much, much, more valuable than money.

The second way to distribute free time is to offer it on a department or section basis. Using this system, you'll tell the employees in a section that they will be offered free time when their section is current or done for the day. There are pros and cons to this. The pro is that employees will try harder to finish their own work if they know they can go home when it's finished. They control their own section more than the whole facility. The con to this method is you might have people going home early from some sections, while others don't get that opportunity as often, or may even have to put in overtime on a frequent basis just to get done. It would stand to reason that rather than spend overtime, it would be more cost efficient to transfer employees from the sections who finished early to the sections that were running behind. These circumstances usually need to be handled on a case-by-case basis, and managers need to be sensitive to issues of fairness, resentment, and quality control in making these decisions.

Which method do we favor? It might surprise you, but we favor the second method. While it doesn't look cost efficient to send people home when you might need overtime in some other sections, it's the best way to nurture the free time program. Some of our methods (perhaps many of our methods!) might appear counterintuitive. Remember the free time junkies? There's a type of employee who rebels against being transferred to another section. You might have a lot of them. These folks get to thinking that if they bust their hump to get their own section done, and then they just get transferred to another section where there are a bunch of zombies, doesn't that mean they're just making more work for themselves? Maybe, they reason, it would be better if they just slowed down during the day to avoid being transferred.

So we come down on the side of option 2. Don't make your employees responsible for managing other sections of your facility. Don't penalize them for getting their own sections done. You're the manager, so you should figure out how to manage the slower sections. You gain considerably more productivity when you make the deal very elementary, and very clear, to your employees. It's simple: when you get your section done, you can go home on free time.

Still not convinced? Consider this fact: Even in facilities filled with free time junkies, there are still enough people who want a full forty hours who are willing to be transferred into the slower sections. A good rule of thumb to always follow as a manager is to do everything possible to allow the banshees to fly. This rule of thumb will serve you well, whether the banshees are banshees of productivity or banshees of free time.

Unions & Simplified Gainsharing

Most managers will frankly admit that they feel it's better to run a union-free facility than one represented by a union. So we begin our union discussion with a paragraph on union avoidance:

We have seen no better union avoidance strategy than Simplified Gainsharing. If you buy into the theory that says the best way to keep unions from your door is to treat your employees with respect and foster good morale, then it's clear that employees will never be interested in a union organizing drive if you're running a successful Simplified Gainsharing program.

PRODUCTIVITY RULE #24

Simplified Gainsharing can be used to transcend union issues, but it's not a panacea.

Now let's get to our discussion of unions and Simplified Gainsharing. Unions are implanted in many facilities at many different levels of cooperation or belligerency. In all cases, Simplified Gainsharing must transcend — and can be used to help the supervisors transcend — the ongoing union issues at the facility.

Before we discuss such transcendence (sounds a little zen-like, no?), allow us to dispense some counsel: Under no circumstances allow Simplified Gainsharing — or any incentive plan for that matter — to become part of contract negotiations. Most unions bless additional bonus monies the company wants to bestow on its employees, such as safety or quality bonuses, and it's best to position productivity incentives under a similar umbrella. The last thing you want is to have to negotiate sliding-scale levels and buyouts every three years. Besides, subjecting the gainshares to the rancor of the negotiating process will jeopardize the good morale benefits of the entire Simplified Gainsharing program.

Facilities that have a good-to-average relationship with their unions should have little difficulty installing Simplified Gainsharing. Is it as easy an installation as at a union-free facility? No, it isn't. It requires more communication at a union facility; and in particular, you need to discuss it with your business agent and stewards before you begin discussing it with your employees. And even before you do that, you should check with your own legal department, of course.

The idea in all union cases is to use Simplified Gainsharing to transcend the union situation in a facility. Regardless of the grievances occurring, regardless of the contract issues, and regardless of the most vocal union supporters, Simplified Gainsharing should always be kept above the fray. For example, "This has nothing to do with union relations, this has to do with you earning as much money as you want." Or, "We've got plenty of other things to fight about, let's make some dough with these sliding scales."

Simplified Gainsharing is not infallible, and it won't cure a bad company/union relationship. And let's point out that there are many facilities with poisonous relationships where Simplified Gainsharing will not even make a dent, particularly since it isn't accepted enough to even be installed; or perhaps the union will demand to negotiate all aspects of incentive plans.

But some of the most interesting Simplified Gainsharing events have occurred at facilities where there is a poisonous relationship with the unions. We want to relate some of the occurrences with Simplified Gainsharing at one company's most volatile union facility.

It was one of the bleakest union/management relationships we've seen. As fate would have it, this facility was also the highest volume facility in its network.

The facility atmosphere was so bad that management contracted an industrial psychologist, a well-respected Ph.D., to come into the facility and study the union/management relationship for a month, in the hopes that the doctor could offer a fresh perspective on how to break through the animosity.

PRODUCTIVITY RULE #25

Even in the worst of union/company relationships, productivity improvement and Simplified Gainsharing can produce worthwhile results.

The doctor conducted the analysis, and unfortunately returned with a bleak ultimatum for the company. Essentially the doctor said the company had just two choices: 1) learn to live with the terrible atmosphere, because the union was in a fight-to-the-death mode, or 2) move the facility.

We wish we could report that Simplified Gainsharing remedied this dire situation, but alas, the only true remedy we've ever seen in such adversarial situations is time itself. Or you could follow the doctor's second option. Still, some interesting occurrences happened at this facility when Simplified Gainsharing was installed. But remember, it's not a panacea.

The first attempt at Simplified Gainsharing at this facility was rebuffed by the union. Management's stance was, "Fine. We're not going to ram this down your throats. Let us know if you're ever ready." Still, the company educated the supervisory staff on the principles of Simplified Gainsharing, and made sure they published the results from the other facilities who were on this incentive plan. Interestingly a couple of the stewards who were not involved in the original rejection began to query the supervisors about the mechanics of Simplified Gainsharing.

The second major attempt by the company to get the program blessed by the union was also rejected. Eight months later, the union attempted to make it part of contract negotiations; the company refused to do this, saying it was traditional that incentive plans were not part of the negotiating process.

But all was not lost.

On the third attempt to install Simplified Gainsharing — two years after the first attempt — the union begrudgingly accepted the installation.

The level of belligerence never decreased, but after two years of hearing tales of employees in other facilities earning two, three, or even four dollars an hour in gainshares, there grew enough of a groundswell within the union ranks at the disgruntled facility that the union could no longer ignore the company's overtures.

Once installed, all was not roses with Simplified Gainsharing. The installation was a lot more contentious than at other facilities; more employees sat on the fence and took a wait-and-see attitude, almost hoping the company would misuse the incentive plan. Of course the greatest fear with Simplified Gainsharing — the fear of the company unilaterally raising standards — was exacerbated. Still, there were banshees here too, just like everywhere else, although they came under considerably more peer pressure than banshees at other facilities. There was always the fear that if individuals greatly extended the bounds of productivity, the company would get the idea that all employees should be going these levels, and unreasonably demand new baselines.

Over the course of the next three years, this facility improved its overall productivity slightly north of 20%, but it was the proverbial leading of the horse to water. In fact, this horse metaphor really doesn't capture the efforts of the supervisory staff and management team to overcome the obstinacy — in reality the horse fell over at the top of the hill, and they had to drag it down to the creek where they force-fed the water into the horse's mouth, massaging its neck muscles to get the horse to swallow. We say all this in case you missed our previous point about Simplified Gainsharing not being a panacea.

However, one amazing occurrence from this facility burned itself into our memories. While touring the building, the corporate sponsor asked the manager why there were no lists of employees who had earned gainshares posted on the various bulletin boards. The manager smiled and replied that there were many stewards earning gainshares, but the supervisors had early on detected an inclination of the stewards to keep this knowledge of their gainshares unpublished.

The corporate sponsor realized it made sense. In most union facilities the stewards are quite meticulous about keeping their productivity slightly below the standards — not far enough below to incur discipline, but never meeting the company's expectations completely. Most stewards live in dread of being called a bootlicker of the company, so you rarely see a steward acting like a productivity banshee. Yet here in the most vehement of union/company relationships, there were stewards earning various levels of gainshares. They just did it anonymously.

The bottom line on this particular installation was that although the amount of employees earning gainshares in this facility never reached the 40% to 50% levels of participation achieved in most other facilities, there was still enough success to make the program worthwhile. The animus never went away, the grievances still poured in as in the past, and nobody ever gathered to praise the company or sing the company theme song; however the gainshares somehow managed to transcend the warfare and earned additional monies for both the company and the employees.

We also know of another facility, one with a similar but less difficult union history, where both standards and an incentive plan were implemented. Following a union-sponsored validation study, the metrics were successfully installed. One of the program's biggest opponents, a union steward, became so enamored with and consequentially involved in the process that he ultimately became a supervisor in the same facility. In general, this approach to productivity improvement and employee recognition can work as well in a union shop as they do in non-union settings.

The Law of Idea Inversion

Have you ever heard the phrase, "Fulton's Folly"? Or how about "Seward's Folly"? Or maybe . . . take your own last name and put it in front of the word "folly" so you can see how it sounds. Ouch. But when you start down the road of Simplified Gainsharing — a system based on giving large raises to certain blue-collar workers — you're going to subject yourself to a certain amount of corporate naysaying.

Both Robert Fulton, the inventor of the steam engine, and William Seward, the Secretary of State who purchased Alaska for $7.2 million, or 2.5 cents per acre, were subjected to ridicule by certain elements of their society. No doubt the proclivity for ridicule came from the potency of their radical changes.

There is a certain tendency in some people to reject any idea that requires change. We call it the Law of Idea Inversion: For every good idea there is an equally compelling opposite idea.

PRODUCTIVITY RULE #26

For every good idea there is an equally compelling opposite idea.

Simplified Gainsharing is a wonderful idea that involves very little capital expense, besides some rudimentary training. It's Plug & Play and often has an ROI of two to four weeks. There's no machine or conveyor or layout design that comes anywhere close to the return on investment like the million-percent range of Simplified Gainsharing. But be prepared for the naysayers.

Your employees will be hitting 10%, 15%, 20%, or 25% levels of productivity increases, and some people in your corporation will begin to wonder why you're paying out those raises. "Why are you paying bonuses for something they should be doing for free — if they're really good workers who have the financial health of the company at heart?" Yeah, sure. But that's nothing! Wait until one of your banshees doubles the baseline rate! That will drive some of the naysayers crazy! "Free money! You're giving away free money!"

Here's the craziness: If you go back to our example on page 10 and extend out the sliding scale in the first example, you'll find that a doubling of productivity will earn the banshee a $4.75 per hour raise. The naysayers will start slapping their foreheads over all the free money you're giving away. You, of course, will tell them to cool their jets, since banshees — who doubled the standard — will earn about $9,880 a year each in incentives. A lot of money, it's true. But they each save you an entire full-time employee, which is worth $35,000 to $40,000 a year in wages and benefits — a more than three-fold return on your money.

You will be absolutely right, and financially very prudent. However, at this point, some naysayer is going to say, "Well, your baseline must have been out of whack and abnormally low for anyone to be able to double the rate."

We hope we don't sound too jaded when we caution you to be prepared for this onslaught. Besides, it's a fair question — maybe the baseline was too low. Even though those metrics could have perpetuated themselves for the next several decades without Simplified Gainsharing. But nevertheless, when the banshees take off, it might be a good time to start thinking about again validating your baseline.

You might need a buyout.

Chapter 5
Buyouts

We hate to admit this, but in the grand world of Simplified Gainsharing, not all is as simple as we would wish. A complex question eventually arises: How do you administer the program in its mature years in order to continue to drive productivity gains into future years?

This is done through buyouts, and since buyouts can often be more art form than policy, we need to discuss this particular art. To begin this discussion, we will propose an ironclad rule for your Simplified Gainsharing program: Nobody gets hurt by Simplified Gainsharing.

This is an extremely important concept, and it includes everyone. You cannot allow the employees to be hurt by it, just as you cannot allow the company to be hurt by improper gainshare ratios. Likewise, you cannot allow your managers to be hurt by it, if they fail to readily understand the principles of Simplified Gainsharing, nor can you allow the supervisors inside your facilities to be hurt if they don't rapidly turn their whole crew into banshees.

The importance of this ironclad rule is simply that if any of the above groups suspects that you're using Simplified Gainsharing to hurt them, and then they see actual proof of it, your program is in severe danger of disintegrating.

So before we get into the nuts and bolts of buyouts, let's examine how these groups of individuals can be hurt by Simplified Gainsharing, or can begin to suspect you're trying to hurt them by wielding it as a hammer. First, let's think about your employees.

PRODUCTIVITY RULE #27

Nobody gets hurt by Simplified Gainsharing.

We've already talked about the below-average or zombie employees who will pine away for the good old days of team incentives. You can't worry about them, because not only were they not hurt in reality, they weren't driving either the old or the new incentive programs. Your deal with this group is simple: you hit the minimums and we'll pay you the base hourly wage. The deal is the same as it always was for these employees.

But there's another big suspicion on many other employees' minds: Are you going to use Simplified Gainsharing to unilaterally raise the standards? In a sense this is the same mantra, with a different spin, that some uninspired accountants drone on and on about concerning superfluous gainshares. Some employees will worry, "If we bust our humps and all hit the higher gainshare levels, you'll come in and raise the standards to the higher levels, then we'll have to bust our humps for nothing the rest of our careers."

So the employees might be worried about the company using Simplified Gainsharing as a device to raise the standards unmercifully. They're worried it's a trick. They've seen some of the company's other decisions in the past concerning their own well-being at work as questionable, and they're suspicious you'll use this new incentive program to trick them into working much harder than they do now.

PRODUCTIVITY RULE #28

Simplified Gainsharing will appear simple to most managers, but some will need special attention to "get it."

The antidote for this fear is to continually publicize your ironclad rule — nobody will be hurt by Simplified Gainsharing . . . and make certain you practice it. This is an essential component of selling the program and a key concept in good, ongoing communications with employees.

But let's move to the other partners in this incentive plan. The next concern is for you to keep the company from being hurt by Simplified Gainsharing. We've spent a lot of time talking about Free Money and the one-third/two-thirds gainshare ratios. In mature Simplified Gainsharing programs — and by mature we mean a program at least twelve to eighteen months old — there's another area you will have to consider if you are to keep the company from getting hurt. That area is the gainshares themselves. Is it reasonable to continue to pay gainshares, for the rest of time, for productivity levels that become second-nature in the facility, or in areas where you have employed new investments to enhance productivity — new machines or forklifts, for example? We think the answer is no, it's not reasonable to pay gainshares for the rest of time at these particular levels. This is why you need a buyout mechanism. When the original equation is changed, the whole system should be adjusted as needed.

However, let's first continue discussing the other groups who can get hurt by Simplified Gainsharing. The next group would be the facility managers.

Managers can get hurt primarily if they do not measure up to corporate expectations for performance. While this is an occupational hazard, we still must be true to our ironclad rule of nobody getting hurt by Simplified Gainsharing. The dynamics are the same for all employees, whether exempt or non-exempt. Just as the blue-collars might spread the word that the company is using Simplified Gainsharing to raise the expectations, so too will managers talk to each other about how the program has been used to pummel them with unrealistic productivity increases and labor savings.

Since we've already noted that we can't expect all managers to be HR gurus, and since we admit that in a group of twenty managers there are bound to be some banshees and some who are below average at these techniques, the corporate sponsor should be prepared to periodically audit the levels of success of the various facilities, then spend some time coaching those managers at the lower end of the success scale. Most managers can be successfully coached to fulfill Simplified Gainsharing productivity goals.

The last group of people who might get hurt by Simplified Gainsharing are the line supervisors.

Even more than with the below-average managers, you should understand that certain supervisors will need to be coached to take full advantage of the Simplified Gainsharing techniques.

Some supervisors understand these principles immediately, and readily wire into the motivational power of sliding scales with no caps. They'll pick up on the Supervisor's Checklist (see Appendix 3), implement quickly, and also invent several new bulletpoints for the checklist. But other supervisors might be a little uncomfortable with such HR-inspired techniques, and put them on the back-burner. It will shortly become evident to the facility manager or superintendent which supervisors are rocking and rolling with the program and which are struggling.

PRODUCTIVITY RULE #29

While supervisors are the most critical group in the facility for the success of Simplified Gainsharing, they are sometimes also the most difficult to coach.

In a sense supervisors are more difficult to coach than managers. With a facility manager, the corporate sponsor can sit in an office alone with the manager and nobody else knows the manager is being coached. But coaching an individual supervisor could very well put a spotlight on the supervisor as someone who isn't exactly fast on the uptake. So the corporate sponsor can't really fly in to meet with individual supervisors.

To avoid unnecessarily singling out a supervisor, the facility managers can have one-on-one talks with supervisors, and the coaching can be performed in a discreet manner without drawing attention to a particular supervisor. Another method is for the manager or superintendent to have weekly Simplified Gainsharing Update meetings, and go to a round-robin format where each supervisor discusses his or her progress with the program. In this manner effective principles and ideas that are really working in the facility come to the forefront, and it can be suggested that all supervisors implement these good ideas. The corporate sponsor can also be invited to periodically attend such meetings, which are both a good way to collect ideas for the rest of the organization and to also disseminate ideas that were discovered in other facilities.

Establishing buyouts

Okay. We think we're finally ready to get into the nuts and bolts of the buyout. We think we've firmly established the maxim that nobody gets hurt by Simplified Gainsharing. If we haven't, please consider re-reading the first part of this chapter.

It's important that everyone understands the principle that nobody gets hurt by Simplified Gainsharing because the concept of buyouts are predicated on the "no hurt" idea. Buyouts are almost more art form than formula. As such, buyouts can be misinterpreted by the workforce as a nefarious, under-handed way to unilaterally raise the standards, if they are not conducted skillfully. But enough of the cautionary hand-wringing.

When exactly do you do a buyout? While there are no set rules, we advise doing it only in facilities with mature Simplified Gainsharing programs. In other words, buyouts are not something that should be done in the beginning of a program. A possible exception to this rule would be if it abruptly becomes clear — in the initial few weeks of a Simplified Gainsharing installation — that the minimum in a section or area is truly off base, and everybody is earning tons of gainshares (we've never encountered the opposite, where nobody can make the gainshares, since the historical minimums would have reflected this situation). We'll discuss the "earning tons" situation shortly in an upcoming section, entitled Startup Buyouts.

PRODUCTIVITY RULE #30

Buyouts are more art form than formula. Proceed more intuitively than mathematically.

Let's assume your program has been up and running for twelve months or so. By that time, 30% to 40% of the employees eligible for the program should be earning some level of gainshares. However, they won't be equally spread throughout all departments of your facility. Instead, there might be some areas where very few or none of the employees are on gainsharing, while other areas will have a high percentage of gainsharers.

In the case where the gainshares coming from an area are anemic, the section baselines should be examined from four angles:

• Are the standards too high or severe?

• Are the employees in these sections all zombies?

• Is the supervisor ineffective?

• Is there some upstream factor that dictates or otherwise impacts performance in a specific section (stocking for pick sections or picking for shipping areas, for example)?

In the fourth instance, performance problems are a symptom of problems somewhere else in the system.

Where a high percentage of employees are on gainshares, a buyout might be in order. A good rule of thumb is when 50% or more of the employees in the area are receiving gainshares, it's probably a good time for a buyout. The first step is to identify areas that meet this criteria, then start the buyout analysis. You can start this by basically asking one question: Do you want to conduct an industrially engineered buyout, or a "do it yourself" buyout? There are good reasons for both.

Do It Yourself Buyouts

Once you determine the section or area in which you want to buy out the existing baseline, you'll want to first determine by what percentage you want to increase the rates in question. But bear in mind, the buyout process is more art form than formula. Not only does nobody get hurt with Simplified Gainsharing, but in the buyout process, the employees have to walk away thinking the company gave them a fantastic deal.

Generally, buyouts range from 5% to 15%, but it is not unknown to go beyond 15% if it is logically supportable. A good clue is to determine where the lower performers are in the section. Will raising the standard automatically throw them into the disciplinary process? If so, this is a group of people you'll be hurting with Simplified Gainsharing. If you proceed with the buyout, these employees are not going to walk away happy; indeed they'll be just the opposite, and will be going around your facility telling everyone, "They want to use gainsharing to trick everyone into working really hard so they can raise the standards on us!" Obviously we don't want to throw employees into automatic discipline by raising a minimum above their current level of performance.

PRODUCTIVITY RULE #31

The employees have to accept the buyout as a wonderful deal for them.

Let's say that a 10% buyout of a baseline rate — say, raising it from 100 to 110 — will still leave everyone in the department close to 110. More than half the employees in this section are earning gainshares, and all the others are already close to 110. It's safe to proceed. But how much do you offer them in the buyout? And does everybody in the section get the buyout bonus, or just the gainsharers?

The answer to the first question is, as much as it takes to make the employees feel like it's a wonderful deal. As a rule of thumb, we use $100 for every 5% you want to buy out, but don't carve this in granite. It's not a solid rule because if your employees don't think it's a great deal, you then need to go to $200 or even $300.

We think we can make a compelling financial case for the buyout, even if you give them $700 or $800 for a 10% buyout.

Let's say your employee is making $10.00 per hour and you raise the standard 10%. The company gains $1.00 per hour in increased productivity. Over the course of the coming year, the company is ahead $2,080 (forty hours times fifty-two weeks) minus the buyout amount. And every year afterwards for the rest of time, the company is ahead $2,080. Not a bad deal for a buyout of $200, $300, $400, or even $800. We think any one of us would be happy to make a capital investment for this kind of ROI.

This example pertains to employees not already on gainshares; for those who are, the new minimum supplants part of their former gainshare rate. In a gainshare program that pays 25 cents for every 5% above standard, the company is gaining 50 cents per hour in this example, or $1,040 per year per employee.

Generally though, gainsharers will figure out how to get back to their original levels of gainshares after a few months. If this becomes the case in the above example, the company will get the full value of a 10% buyout because the gainsharers will end up at 20% above the old standard (10% above the new).

Once you have your numbers in mind — and for the sake of this example, let's use a 10% buyout, worth $200 gross for each employee in the section — it's safe to begin approaching the employees.

But don't start with a group meeting. Instead, begin the process by having the area supervisor approach one of the banshees to discuss the possibility of a buyout: "Hey Fred, I've noticed that most of the folks in this section have been hitting on gainsharing pretty regularly for the past several months. I don't know if you remember that buyout provision in the Simplified Gainsharing plan document, but there might be a way for you folks to get a sizeable bonus check."

PRODUCTIVITY RULE #32

Conduct the buyout with an eye toward scuttlebutt (i.e., take advantage of the ever-present rumor mill). It's advantageous to your bottom line to have many employees in your facility talking about what a great deal you delivered in the buyout.

It's a good practice to float a few trial balloons with the banshees and some of the other employees who are getting gainshares. Don't worry if the process takes a couple of weeks; as we mentioned earlier, this is more art form than formula. Why do banshees bite hard on this? Because $200 is cash in their hands, a form of free money. And they know they have more depth to their own productivity. If so, they can continue to earn gainshares after the sliding scales have shifted higher.

But let's say you've done your due diligence, and you've discovered that the majority of the employees in the section are interested in hearing more about buyouts. Word of mouth has passed the idea around the area, and it appears the buyout idea is striking your workforce as favorable. Now is the time to have the supervisor begin floating some numbers to some of the banshees. Remember, we would want to offer them at least $200 for a 10% raise in the standards, so your supervisor should start with this figure.

If $200 is accepted as a good deal by the banshees, float the number to the rest of the people in the section. On the other hand, if $200 isn't igniting the imaginations of any of the banshees, go to $300 or even $400. But be careful about going too far, because whatever you eventually arrive at as an exciting deal, this number will most likely set a precedent for buyouts in your facility. Not that $400 for a 10% perpetual gain is very onerous, but make sure you're then prepared to live with a $200 payout for every 5% bump far into the future.

Time is not of the essence. Float the dollar amount of the buyout bonus checks around the department for several weeks if that's what it takes for everyone to get comfortable with the idea. Give employees time to spend the money in their minds. Often the buyout amounts are received coolly on first hearing, but after a couple of weeks, people warm up to the idea.

Also make sure that the majority of employees in the buyout section end up embracing the deal as a very generous one. This is important. You want them to see the buyout as generous because they'll spread the word around your facility that the company is extremely fair in the manner in which it conducts Simplified Gainsharing. When you're at this point, have a department meeting and consummate the deal. Ideally you want your first buyout to go so fortuitously that employees from other sections approach other supervisors to query about how they too can get one of these buyout bonuses.

Lastly, the buyout bonus is bestowed on every employee in the section where the standards are being raised — not only the gainsharers. The fairness of this method is simply that everyone in the section is going to have to live with the new standard, not just the gainsharers, and also, you want everyone in the section talking to other employees about how fair the company was with these bonuses.

Industrially Engineered Buyouts

While there are advantages to do it yourself buyouts, there's another way to conduct the buyouts. Bring in the industrial engineers.

As we mentioned in Chapter 2, the danger of using industrial engineers (IEs) is that if your engineers use a 100% expression of the baseline, your employees might view the time and motion studies as science, and put a psychological cap on their own performance. As a reminder of what they might think: If science says the standard should be 100, isn't it scientifically impossible to do 200? Or 300? Using a "zero" baseline avoids this problem.

A better way is to introduce the IEs to the workforce as "Buyout Engineers" or "Improvement Managers." Explain to the workforce that the Simplified Gainsharing program has been running for over a year now, and the company is considering offering bonus checks for re-adjusting the baseline rates. So in order to determine what would be fair to the employees and fair to the company, these time and motion experts will be conducting studies in your departments to determine if there is justification for the bonus checks.

It's a good idea to float into the workforce some elementary formulas for determining the buyout levels, such as $100 for every 5%, or $200 for every 5%. If your employees start counting their money and looking forward to sizeable bonus checks, they will be much more accepting of the buyout engineers. Indeed, they might even encourage the IEs to be more liberal in their recommendations to raise the standards. This is a much better frame of mind for your employees than for them to fear that the company is trying to unilaterally raise the rates.

PRODUCTIVITY RULE #33

Even when you use industrial engineers, buyouts are more art form than formula.

It's also important to have your industrial engineers trained in the principles of Simplified Gainsharing, and schooled in how you want them to interact with the employees in the sections they will be studying. The ideal situation is for the employees and the industrial engineers to see each other as both working toward setting a fair buyout level.

While our next statement might be anathema to industrial engineers, it still needs to be brought up again: buyouts are more art form than formula. More art than science.

Done correctly, buyouts should have your employees singing your praises due to the generosity of your offer. You know you've done it right when you have employees from other sections coming up to you to ask why you didn't do a buyout in their area.

Capital Expense Buyouts

We also need to consider the counterintuitive elements around the Capital Expense Buyouts.

What do you do about Simplified Gainsharing metrics if you spend $1 million in capital improvements with an 18-month return on investment, much of which is expected to come in the form of improved productivity? Clearly performance expectations will have to be raised, and the Simplified Gainsharing sliding scales will need to be adjusted upward, won't they?

Of course. But there are good ways to do this, and there are bad ways. The best way is to do it in a manner that insures the success of your $1 million capital investment.

PRODUCTIVITY RULE #34

Maintain the current sliding scale structure for the first few months following a capital improvement investment. Then offer a buyout.

Let's start with the bad way — you can take a totally objective approach and be completely rational with your workforce, but suffer from a decrease in morale. For example, you could objectively explain to your workforce that the capital investment will produce a 25% increase in efficiency, so starting at the implementation of the capital improvements, the sliding scales will now begin at a level 25% above the current start.

This is completely fair, and an objective stance to take, but we can almost guarantee you that even though the explanation is completely rational, there will be segments of the workforce that will perceive it as unfair and an attempt to cheat workers out of their gainshares. If that occurs, the 25% gain in productivity you anticipated will be a long time coming, and the capital improvement may very well deteriorate your Simplified Gainsharing program and flatten morale.

Consider a better way to implement a capital improvement. Like the other method, go through a lengthy and effective communication program to explain to the employees why you anticipate a 25% gain in productivity. Once they understand your figures, tell the workforce that you'll run the current sliding scales from their current starting points for the next two months (or perhaps three if there is a training curve involved in making the capital improvement work) and then you'll conduct a buyout by issuing buyout bonus checks. Only then would you readjust the sliding scales.

We would suggest that if you do indeed achieve your 25% gain in the first two to three months after your implementation, then issue bonus checks of $200 to $300. While this check amount is less than our formula of $100 for every 5% raise of the standard, it will be perceived as extraordinarily fair since you allowed the sliding scales to run unadjusted in the months directly following the implementation of the capital improvement.

This method might appear counterintuitive in an accounting sense, but it is a more profitable practice in reality since it greatly increases the chances of a slam dunk implementation and ROI for your capital investment. Especially when compared to the opposite method where you risk negatively impacting your employee morale and effectiveness of your incentive plan.

Another good way to achieve gains from capital improvements while maintaining a robust Simplified Gainsharing program is to use the "Step Up" method. This method is discussed in detail in Appendix 2, Metrics & Baselines.

Start-up Buyouts

Sometimes during the start-ups of Simplified Gainsharing, we see a miscue in one of the facility metrics.

A typical miscue will go along these lines: Within the first week or two of the start-up, a section will abruptly double its productivity, and all, or nearly all, of the section's employees will be at a rate to earn astounding levels of gainshares. How does this happen? Was Simplified Gainsharing such a great idea that it motivated everyone to abruptly start working at 100% above the baseline?

As much as we would like to take credit for these great gains, Simplified Gainsharing has never motivated whole departments to instantly double productivity (although it can indeed achieve this over the course of several years). But if Simplified Gainsharing isn't responsible for this phenomenon, then what is?

There are several reasons for these miscues: perhaps the baseline hadn't been accurately monitored in the past, or the measure had recently been invented or measurements recently begun, or a new method of tabulation has been put into place, or the employees discovered a new and easy way to make production. Whatever the reason, the metric needs to be quickly adjusted, or the employees in other departments will conclude you're not running a fair and level playing field.

PRODUCTIVITY RULE #35

In some start-ups, miscues in minimum expectations instantly surface. Care should be taken to always maintain good morale in resolving these issues.

We suggest starting by calling a department meeting and simply asking the employees why they think the department has abruptly leaped ahead in productivity. It might sound like a simplistic approach, but most times the employees will sheepishly respond with something like, "We wondered how long it would take before you asked us this." And the reasons will quickly bubble to the top. If the event is taken good-naturedly by the company and the employees, we suggest you tell the employees that you'll give them credit for what occurred in the past measurements, but in all fairness the metric needs to be adjusted going forward.

In most cases, the employees can tell you where to fairly set the new minimum in this situation. However if you're not comfortable in doing this, then bring in the "Buyout Engineers" (industrial engineers) to determine what's fair for both the employees and the company.

In those cases where the initial meeting is not going good-naturedly, you might have to conduct a buyout in accordance with the descriptions provided in the previous sections. In all cases, the company should seek to defuse the situation as smoothly as possible; it's important to maintain good morale since there is so much at stake concerning the overall financial gains for the organization.

Audacious Buyouts

Buyouts are one of the prime tools in your toolbox to construct, then achieve, the ultimate audacious goal for your facilities — the doubling of productivity.

You can use the following method to take buyouts to this ultimate level. We call it the "Audacious Buyout," and it's not for the faint of heart, nor is it for a manager who is a buyout virgin. In other words, it needs to be practiced only by managers who are comfortable with the entire buyout techniques and who have successfully performed a number of them.

Bear in mind, the worst thing you can do with a buyout is give your workforce the impression that you are unilaterally — and painfully for them — raising the standards. Always remember: No one gets hurt by Simplified Gainsharing.

Here's how you do the Audacious Buyout.

Step 1. Pick your best department or section in a facility, one where 90% of the employees have already gone through a buyout, and one that is predominantly populated by banshees and employees with positive attitudes. Once you pick the section, send in a supervisor to start talking to the banshees about a "Super Buyout."

Why do we now call it a Super Buyout? Frankly, we thought "Super Buyout" would sound better to your employees than "Audacious Buyout," but we wanted you to understand we're tying it into the Audacious Goal Program, where it can be used to help double productivity.

Here's how it works:

PRODUCTIVITY RULE #36

Be Audacious. Start with a 25% goal over the current average in the best section of your best facility.

Pick a super productivity goal for the section. Remember, this is a section where you've already performed a buyout or two, so it will be a section where you believe there's very little "fat" in the standards and productivity performance. We think at this juncture you should at least pick a 25% goal.

Twenty-five percent! Are we nuts? How can you get 25% additional productivity out of a section that is already at the top of the all-time performance lists?

The answer is there are few boundaries when it comes to human performance.

Step 2. Convince the section supervisor that a 25% increase (or whatever goal you select) is a feasible idea.

A real-life story would go a long way toward shoring up everyone involved, eh? But before we deliver a story, allow us to put forth another one of our counterintuitive theories: Banshees will always find ways to be banshees. Indeed, they can't help themselves. However, don't get the idea that the Audacious Buyout is simple. It's not; it's an intricate maneuver.

Now, on with the story:

At a Simplified Gainsharing facility, the supervisor of the best department determined to use the Audacious Buyout for his third buyout in the past eighteen months. In a strategy session with the facility superintendent, he determined that he could sell the idea of a 25% raise in the standard for $800. The superintendent thought he was nuts — they had already bought out 20% in the past eighteen months — but was willing to allow the supervisor to start floating the idea around his department. After all, a 25% buyout in a ten-person crew would enable the facility to shed two employees by attrition — this would be worth $70,000 a year to the facility. So this audacious idea certainly had the interest of the facility's management.

The supervisor thought he had an opportunity to reach for the brass ring because he had noticed something from the past two buyouts: Each time he thought he had raised the standards to the high end of human performance, he saw that within two to three months, the banshees were back earning gainshares again; and within three to four months, they were back to their former levels of gainshares, even though it meant fully re-defining the definition of superlative performance in the department. He saw that the banshees figured out ways to work much smarter, they developed unique shortcuts (prior to Simplified Gainsharing they really had no percentage in developing shortcuts), and they were a lot more focused on their work, intent on earning the highest possible gainshare.

PRODUCTIVITY RULE #37

Banshees will always find ways to be banshees.

We should probably point out at this juncture that this department was already the highest performing department in the whole network — it was already the best in the country!

The supervisor decided to test the high side of the curve; but first he had to convince the superintendent that $800 was an appropriate number for a buyout. He persuaded his boss that where it was certainly above the $100 for 5% formula, it was indeed appropriate for a department that had already gone through two previous buyouts.

After he had the superintendent's approval for an $800 buyout, our supervisor then had to structure his plan to raise the standards by 25%.

He began with the best banshee in the department, an employee who was already hitting a 35% gainshare. The supervisor floated the idea, "You know how we had a couple of buyouts with darn good buyout checks in the past year and a half? What would you say if I could get the company to cough up a $800 bonus?" On his first pass with the idea, he met with a little skepticism; the banshee wondered if 25% was reaching too far.

The supervisor approached it logically, "Maybe. We're not going to do something that you guys think is too far of a reach. But you're already at the 35% level, so a 25% buyout wouldn't be out of the question for you. And $800 is a pretty big deal — it's almost two weeks pay."

It took about a week of periodic, short discussions for the original banshee to warm up to the idea. But once he did, he started to convince the other banshees in the department. Our supervisor was well on his way. Over the next two weeks, our supervisor was able to convince eight of the ten employees who would be involved in the buyout.

There was one final big nut to crack in the pursuit of the 25% raise in the standard. Two of the employees in the section were average employees. They were above the disciplinary levels, but not earning a gainshare; in fact in the past eighteen months, they had never earned even a single gainshare, but always managed to stay above the disciplinary levels of all the past buyouts. So although the other eight employees in the section were either above the levels the new standard would establish or were confident they could achieve the 25% increase, these two average employees would be thrown into immediate discipline if the standard were raised.

PRODUCTIVITY RULE #38

Once a buyout bonus number attracts a banshee or two in the department, nurse the concept along, until ways are found to satisfy all the employees.

Still, two weeks' pay was a big plum for the other employees, and a certain amount of bad blood sprang up between the gainsharers and the two average employees. At last the supervisor thought of a solution where nobody would get hurt. If the department did indeed raise its standards 25%, instead of ten people, the department could do the same work with only eight people. Of course all ten would receive the $800 buyout, but the company was buying the ability to raise the standards 25% with the eight gainsharers, while with the two average employees, the company was buying the right to move them to another section in the facility where an Audacious Buyout was not being considered, and they could produce at levels above the standards.

We should note that this math worked because the banshees projected to the supervisor they could soon raise their own productivity after the buyout in order to continue earning gainshares at the same levels as before the buyout. This is how two employees were able to be moved out of the department.

So in the end, nobody got hurt. The company raised the standards 25%, and all the employees got a bonus worth nearly two weeks pay. And the most interesting part of this story? After two or three months, the banshees did indeed return to similar levels of gainshares as they were making before the Audacious Buyout.

As you recall, the first two steps in the Audacious Buyout were:

Step 1 – Pick your best department.

Step 2 – Convince the supervision.

Now, after dissecting the example we've just discussed, we can add the following steps:

Step 3 – Determine an audacious amount for the buyout (in the example, the supervisor used $800 for a 25% buyout).

Step 4 – Start the buyout discussions with the banshees rather than a departmental meeting.

Step 5 – Be patient if the banshees or anyone else pushes back (remember, we all have the tendency to spend money in our minds, so the Audacious Buyout will appear more doable after a few days).

Step 6 – Get buy-in from the rest of the department, after the banshees are comfortable with the numbers (the banshees will help convince everyone else).

Step 7 – Be creative if necessary (in the example, two employees needed to be transferred to avoid falling below the new minimum expectations).

Step 8 – Never hurt anyone by the Audacious Buyout process (in the long run, this rule will keep your whole program more profitable).

Buyout Audits

Our final point concerning buyouts: Someone from corporate needs to conduct buyout audits.

An easy way to choose buyout candidates comes from having a corporate person track all departments in all facilities. It will quickly become apparent which facilities are paying out the highest levels of gainshares. A review or buyout audit can then be conducted at that facility, where departments with 50% or more of the employees earning gainshares can be identified. If you use a corporate IE for this assignment, the IE is then already on site if time studies need to be performed as a prelude to the buyout.

Harkening back to our point of how we shouldn't expect facility managers to be HR gurus, we can't expect them all to latch onto the nuances of buyouts. Also, because the buyout levels need to vary from facility to facility or even from section to section within facilities, clear-cut formulas cannot be published, simply because they don't exist.

PRODUCTIVITY RULE #39

A corporate person needs to monitor the Simplified Gainsharing performance of all facilities. Periodic buyout audits need to be conducted.

For example, back on the case study of the supervisor conducting the Audacious Buyout at the 25% level, an employee from another section in that facility could very well stand up at a facility meeting and ask the facility manager why he hadn't received an $800 bonus check when his minimums were bought out. The employee might even ask, "Wasn't there a $100 for 5% rule of thumb? So how did they get eight C-notes for theirs? What's this all about?"

Potential answers could be: 1) We constantly strive to do what's fair for the employees while also being fair to the company. In this case, the degree of difficulty warranted the level of buyout, and both the company and this section's employees arrived at mutually acceptable numbers. Or 2) On the surface, it appears to be an overly generous amount, but remember this is the third buyout in less than 18 months, and over this period of time the section has increased their minimums by 50%. In our eyes, this outstanding performance warrants $800. Remember, too, this section is not just good, it's head and shoulders above all the similar sections in the entire national network. When your section arrives at these levels, come and see us — we have the eight C-notes for you, too!

As you can see, there's a certain amount of daily creativity required for the implementation of buyouts. It's a good idea to create a corporate position for someone to monitor the performance of all facilities on Simplified Gainsharing and conduct periodic gainshare audits. This might be a good job for a corporate industrial engineer, although it should be one who can wire into the more artistic or negotiating side of buyout theory. The wisdom of using a corporate person is: You can standardize buyout best practices across the network while assuring the company that baselines are continuing to progress upward in all facilities as a consequence of the gainshares being paid out.

Chapter 6
Turnover

We've covered many benefits of Simplified Gainsharing — productivity, quality, antidote to boredom — but there's one more benefit that will completely change the complexion of your workforce. Turnover evaporates.

Making your turnover rates dwindle to single digits is an important component in your own workforce resurrection. Installing Simplified Gainsharing in a facility changes the nature of its compensation nearly instantly. Instead of paying employees for putting in a certain amount of time, the facility now pays higher wages for higher performance based on a sliding scale with no caps. This changes everything.

One of the main reasons banshees don't do more than what they actually do during the years prior to Simplified Gainsharing is because they're surrounded by many of their peers who ask them, "Why are you so nuts? The company doesn't pay you anything more for going beyond the standards, so why do you keep doing it? Are you a brown-noser, or what?" These are hard questions for the banshees to answer, even though it's in their blood to always perform ahead of their peers.

PRODUCTIVITY RULE #40

Dramatic improvement of a workforce's turnover is an automatic consequence of a Simplified Gainsharing installation.

With Simplified Gainsharing, this whole equation changes. Now the banshees are paid exactly what they think they are worth. And better — the banshees determine themselves what they are worth. Shortly this spreads throughout the entire workforce. Workers who were average prior to the Simplified Gainsharing installation now realize that a simple 5% uptick in their own performance produces a 25-cent raise for them. There is now a very clear answer to the question, "Why do more?"

If you're a banshee in this environment, and you learn how to make several dollars more per hour, you are now holding what might very well be the best blue-collar job in your community. Why go anywhere else? Not to mention the feeling of freedom when you, as a blue-collar worker, exercise such control over your own wages.

One of our favorite examples of improvement is a company that moved its network turnover rates from 44% (pretty horrendous) to 7% in less than three years after installing Simplified Gainsharing. While it's difficult to put a number to the value of such turnover reduction (although we'll give it a shot shortly), it's incontrovertible that such a reduction in turnover is clearly in the interest of the facility. Having a stable and highly cross-trained workforce is an important competitive advantage.

There's a theory of management called topgrading, which, in a nutshell, advocates hiring only the very best people for each job. But whether it's management or blue-collar, this task of hiring only the best is not an easy one to accomplish, and it requires quite a bit of interviewing.

Wouldn't it be better to take the workforce you already have, and turn it into one that includes the best possible employees? With the installation of Simplified Gainsharing, you're well on your way to developing a workforce that is unparalleled in your industry. As your employees earn more per hour using this approach, they'll drive up your productivity and improve your quality rates. When half of your workforce hits its groove at an appropriate gain-share level, you'll see that morale has improved and turnover has begun a steady decrease, since the employees on gainshares come to understand they now have one of the best jobs in town. And as turnover decreases, cross-training automatically increases — all of this moves you in the direction of topgrading your workforce.

We said we'd take a crack at putting a dollar value to improved turnover. Human Resource manuals often put the cost of turnover at two, or even three, times the employee's annual compensation. To our ears, this sounds a tad high for blue-collar workers, but one could make a case that when you put a dollar value to all the intangibles, it adds up to some big numbers.

Using a more conservative approach, one network's corporate staff polled their facility managers with a request to put a dollar value to all the actual expenses of interviewing, hiring, and training a new blue-collar employee, including all the pre-employment testing. Averaging the response of twenty facility managers, the staff tallied the turnover cost for one blue-collar employee as $2,500.

While $2,500 isn't exactly an earthshaking number, it did open some eyes in this particular network that was turning over more than 600 employees per year. When you do the multiplication, turnover was conservatively costing this network $1.5 million per year, and probably considerably more if all the soft costs were taken into consideration. The good news is that Simplified Gainsharing produced a 60% improvement in the turnover rates two years after installation — such improvement being worth $900,000 per year to the company going forward.

Chapter 7
Questions & Answers

As we've discussed these Simplified Gainsharing principles with facility managers over the years, a potpourri of questions have arisen, so we've included them here, before going into more detail about managing a Simplified Gainsharing program.

Question: What type of productivity increases should I expect after a Simplified Gainsharing installation in my facility?

Answer: It really depends on the motivational skills of the facility's management team. Normally, Simplified Gainsharing starts slowly in the first month, then grows with each successive month. Most facilities can expect to see 50% to 60% of their employees participating after the first year. As the program matures, and as non-participating employees leave the company, these percentages of participation will reach 80% to 90%. At such levels of participation, the overall productivity of the facility should attain a 20% to 30% increase; but it is heavily dependent on whether facility management uses the hours saved to avoid hiring during attrition or to complete projects within the facility.

While it's certainly not the norm, we believe the facility manager should assume the audacious goal of a 100% productivity increase during the five years following the Simplified Gainsharing installation. Some facilities have used Simplified Gainsharing as a springboard to obtain this lofty goal. We discuss the methods used by this handful of managers — "Banshee Managers," if you will — in Part Two of *Warehouse Productivity*.

Question: When installing the sliding scales in a section or department, should you start at the disciplinary point (minimum expectations), or should you instead start at the departmental productivity averages, which are generally above the minimums?

Answer: It's done either way. Departmental averages are the fairest start for the company in the eyes of many accountants. But starting at the disciplinary point is a good way to "salt" the program and get it off to a good start. We favor the latter because an inspired manager keeps an eye on the long-range goals of Simplified Gainsharing where the future buyouts move all the departmental averages far ahead of both the disciplinary points and beginning averages.

Question: Should you install Simplified Gainsharing in a facility that is struggling with productivity problems, or should you wait until all the low-hanging fruit has first been gathered by other means?

Answer: This is somewhat akin to the prior question. The answer is similar: Your accountants might be more comfortable with waiting until all the low-hanging fruit has been picked up. But do you really want to wait a couple of years for that to happen? And what if it doesn't happen? We favor jumping right in. You'll see how Simplified Gainsharing is the premier harvester of low-hanging fruit; and if you use the buyout principles in the described manner, you'll be able to drive your facility's productivity far, far beyond its current levels.

Question: If you have a choice of several facilities, is it best to start Simplified Gainsharing in the best one or the worst?

Answer: It's best to start Simplified Gainsharing in the facility that has the managerial and supervisory team that's most skillful at motivating employees. This staff will most likely be found in the most productive facility in your network. Since the first installation is always seen as a pilot, it's important for the future success of the network installation that the first Simplified Gainsharing facility is successful.

If you're going to take a shot at doubling your network productivity, then you'll need a pace-setting facility to lead the way for the rest of your network, as discussed in Part Two. All the more reason to start Simplified Gainsharing in the facility with the most skillful staff.

Question: When employees start earning gainshares, shouldn't there be restrictions so that only those employees who also have good attendance or a lack of disciplinary infractions are eligible for these gainshares? Why pay bonuses to those employees who are counterproductive in other areas?

Answer: While it's understandable to want to reward only those employees who are exemplary in all areas, you don't want to kill any golden geese. Many employees are going to be suspicious of any new incentive program in the beginning, so you want to achieve as many victories as you can after you launch Simplified Gainsharing. If an employee decides to test run the program and achieves, say, a 15% gainshare level in the first month, then sees the gainsharing raise taken away because of an attendance infraction, the employee will sour on the program. Worse, the employee will then sour other employees on the program. We believe it's for the greater good if the only "string attached" is the quality qualifier. Most employees find it reasonable to have a qualifier for quality; but many employees find it unfair to lose their gainshares for other reasons.

Question: Many of our employees float from one section to another during the course of a day or week. How do you determine their productivity levels on the sliding scales? Do you need a sliding scale for each place they work during the month? Won't this record-keeping drive us crazy?

Answer: Yes, it may indeed drive you nuts. We recommend assigning a "home base" for each employee, so when individuals transfer between sections to help balance the day's work flow, you won't have to track them in multiple sliding scales. Also, this is most fair for the employee, since each worker develops a proclivity for the area in which he or she spends the most time during the month, or the area to which he or she is assigned. Most facilities look at where the employee spends 51% of his or her time during the month, and call that area the home base. But if you have a floater or lead person who isn't able to log 51% in any given area, be careful that you don't penalize this worker. We suggest you reach an agreement with the employee on which area can be used as a home base.

Question: For the next month after the employee earns a gainshare level, do you pay the gainshare raises for all hours worked, or just those worked in the home base?

Answer: Gainshare raises should be paid for all hours worked in the following month, including overtime hours. The record-keeping required to vary hourly pay rates per employee would certainly drive you nuts. Besides, employees will see this deal as the most fair, especially since it's easy to understand: You hit the levels in one month, then you'll get the raise for all hours worked the following month. Remember, your goal is to reach the buyout points, continuously raising productivity, so you should be ready to salt the path to these buyout and audacious buyout levels.

Question: Our network has been on Simplified Gainsharing for two years, and we've seen our average wage in the network balloon 25% from where we started the program. Is this good?

Answer: In most cases, it's very good. The network average wage will go up considerably as more and more employees participate in Simplified Gainsharing and earn higher and higher gainshare levels. The corporate staff should see a corresponding decrease in the amount of FTEs employed in the network. Clearly as productivity goes up, fewer employees are needed to produce the same throughput. So where the network's average wage goes up, the network's labor ratio will go down.

In the unlikely case where your network's labor ratio is not decreasing in a corresponding manner to the increase of your average wage, you might have a severe case of the "Project Junkies." Please read the chapter that describes this corporate malady in Part Two.

Question: Our banshees were working considerably above their departments' averages before we installed Simplified Gainsharing. Aren't we now paying them gainshares for what they were doing for free in the past?

Answer: Yes. To some extent this is true, you're now paying for something you were getting for free in the past. But hang in there. We're certain the banshees will kick it into high gear and drive their department's averages far above where they were in the past. When the banshees realize that the higher they take their individual productivity, the bigger the raise they get the following month, the sky becomes the limit to their future productivity. And this is a phenomenon you would never have seen in the days before Simplified Gainsharing.

Question: Are you worried about a fatigue factor or safety risks? Our banshees are going at top speed all day, and appear to be worn out at the end of the day. Some banshees are even running at certain points. We're concerned this could lead to accidents.

Answer: The fatigue part of the question can really be answered by each individual banshee. Clearly, we all pace ourselves to adequately handle the work we assign ourselves. Many banshees bite off a tad more than they can chew, then speed up to attain their goals. The latter effort leads to fatigue, but the banshees solve it by either physically adapting to the pace of their goals over time or adjusting their goals to fit the overall endurance of their bodies. In short, it's a process we all — even paper pushers like us — apply to the demands of our jobs.

The other part of your question requires a more serious management approach. Safety can never be compromised in the pursuit of gainshares. It's not fair to the banshee if supervision allows running or unsafe practices, nor is it fair to the surrounding employees. Supervisors must manage through these problems, and counsel any employee they spot doing something unsafe.

However, at the risk of being coy, we must ask, "Aren't these good problems to have?" Most facilities spend their time planning how to get that next 5% increase in productivity, not planning how to slow their employees down.

Question: Does the Fair Labor Standards Act (FLSA) require Simplified Gainsharing raises to be taxed differently than the employee's regular tax rate? Or are gainshares to be treated as bonuses and taxed accordingly?

Answer: No, to both questions. Since Simplified Gainsharing gainshares are part of an employee's regular wage, your payroll department does not have to make distinct calculations because the gainshare raise is used for all hours worked (including overtime) in the following month. Also, gainshares are considered part of regular raises, and as such are not taxed at the bonus rates, but taxed at the employee's regular tax rate.

Question: We like the idea of Simplified Gainsharing, but some of your ideas may not work well in our culture. How closely do we have to follow your outline to be successful?

Answer: Over the course of the years while rolling out Simplified Gainsharing programs, we learned that it's better to modify the rules to embrace the subculture of a facility than it is to jam rules down the throats of managers, supervisors, or employees. It's no doubt better to pick your battles, or be discerning on when to capitulate and when to stand strong. For instance, there are certain rules of Simplified Gainsharing that we hold to be inviolate. Such rules are:

• Maintain sliding scales with no caps, based on 5% incremental levels.

• Always strive for individual performance gainshares, and go to small teams only as a last resort.

• Keep the gainshare payout cycles as short as reasonably possible (we generally use a month) so there's a clear understanding of the effort/reward relationship on the employees' part.

• Pay the gainshares as hourly raises, not as lump sum bonuses.

• Don't qualify the gainshares with anything beyond quality. Don't use attendance, safety or disciplinary offenses to disqualify gainshares.

• Tie in managerial and supervisory bonuses directly to the Simplified Gainsharing engine.

• Don't hurt anyone with Simplified Gainsharing or buyouts.

Chapter 8
Managing Simplified Gainsharing

You successfully implemented a Simplified Gainsharing program, and six months later you have 30% to 40% of a facility's employees earning a gainshare. Everything is great, and that facility should be showing marked improvement to its labor ratio. Right?

Not always.

Not every facility manager is created the same, or more precisely, not every facility manager is aiming for the same goals. Most facility managers are aiming at their budgets; a couple of facility managers are aiming at being number one in productivity in the network; and we must admit there are a couple of facility managers at the lower end of the spectrum who might cause corporate to sometimes wonder what exactly it is they're aiming at. In short, the ratios of banshees and zombies in the managerial groups are similar to those in the supervisory and employee groups, although managers might be a lot more clever at shielding themselves from such characterizations.

PRODUCTIVITY RULE #41

Drive out excess FTEs achieved by the productivity improvements of Simplified Gainsharing. The corporate sponsor needs to be aware of the proclivity of some facility managers to fuel their own projects.

Simplified Gainsharing produces tons of excess hours within the facility, but not all facility managers use these hours to enhance the labor ratios or improve the profit picture. For example, if five employees all obtain a 20% gainshare — which of course indicates a 20% increase in productivity — you would have a forty-hour-per-week reduction in the labor needed to do the work of these five employees (eight hours from each employee).

What the company needs from the situation is for the facility to shed a Full Time Equivalent (FTE). The company would save $30,000 to $40,000 in wages and benefits from an FTE, while paying out a dollar per hour to each of the five employees, or $10,400 in overall gainshares. This is well within the one-third/two-thirds payout formula.

However this doesn't always happen. In fact, we're sad to say that it doesn't happen the majority of the time. What gives?

The answer lies in the above proportion of banshees in any given group of human beings. The banshee facility managers will shed the FTE in a minute, because this is the way to use Simplified Gainsharing to drive their productivity numbers higher and higher. But when you move farther into the group of network facility managers — and farther away from the banshees — you hit a large group of facility managers who use Simplified Gainsharing (or any other incentive plan, for that matter) for a dual purpose. These managers use Simplified Gainsharing to attain their facility budgets for the year, but they don't go very far past that point. Instead of driving toward the heights of potential productivity, they use the greater chunk of gained hours to fuel projects within the facility.

You often see the same phenomenon with process improvements or engineering design upgrades. Not all hours saved make it to the bottom line.

Chapter 9
Project Junkies

When some facility managers begin to see a reduction in the hours needed to process the daily production, they begin to spend these excess hours on their own wish lists.

Perhaps they'll use these hours to catch up on cycle counts or enhance their bin-sizing efforts, or pour them into upticking their housekeeping, or any of a thousand other projects. Of course, what corporate would like to see is a rapid shedding of FTEs, which can be accomplished by an increase in the free-time allocations, or a decrease or halt to the hiring process, or even a layoff (although you have to be careful to keep a layoff separated from gainshares — remember, nobody gets hurt by Simplified Gainsharing).

But wait a minute! What's wrong with using these hours to increase future productivity? Shouldn't facility managers always keep an eye toward improving productivity? Shouldn't they always be investing in the future?

Yes, of course. But let's go down this path: Just as Will Rogers never met a person he didn't like, facility managers have never met a project they couldn't redesign to their own liking. Scratch any facility manager, and you'll find four or five pet projects that are waiting for the right moment or the right gift of labor hours. All facility managers are waiting for that time of the year when business slows down for a little while, allowing them to jump on whatever project has made it to the top of their pet project list.

PRODUCTIVITY RULE #42

Beware of excess hours that never leave the facility. Excess FTEs do not equal $ savings, and may not represent improvements unless they go away.

Somewhere in the second or third month of Simplified Gainsharing, facility managers realize they have hit the mother lode of extra labor hours. "This is great! Not only can I move the labor ratios a little in the right direction, and make my budget, but I can also re-design the shipping dock the way I've always wanted."

But again — what's wrong with using these hours to increase future productivity?

The problem is most managers never hit the bottom of the well — the project idea well. This water flows forever. If you don't believe us, think of your own career. Have you ever not had an idea? Have you never — at any point in your career — had a project you were dying to try?

And this phenomenon creates a problem for corporate — the company never sees the full benefit of the incentive plan it's funding.

Facility managers could easily suck up the majority of labor hours created by Simplified Gainsharing, while the corporate types are sitting in the ivory tower wondering why the labor ratios are not improving in relation to the gainshares being paid out.

Before we describe the cure, let's first discuss the most extreme form of the malady — that of the Project Junkie. Bear in mind that we trust we're not appearing deleterious when we call some managers Project Junkies, for we don't believe they're doing this as a conscious attempt to hurt the company's financials. We say all this with great respect for facility managers, but like a form of substance abuse, the head-rush of creativity can lead to a misguided dependency on projects. Before you know it, you're hooked.

PRODUCTIVITY RULE #43

Tracking systems for incentive plans need to take into account where all the hours are going that are generated from the improvements.

As one project leads to the next, the more dependent managers begin to realize that the projects buffer them from the demands of corporate to increase productivity. In the worst cases, it gets insidious: the facility manager creates a nine-month major re-layout and bin-sizing project, gets corporate approval, then quickly realizes at the beginning of the project that the facility's overall productivity decreases are due to all the hours being put into the re-layout. The manager explains to corporate that the hours being poured in the project are adversely impacting productivity, but when the project is completed, the facility is going to zoom.

Most corporate staffs will buy into this logic, although some might ask for an accounting of all project hours so they can be deducted from the productivity calculations. We might sound a little jaded, but the hours, when reported by the facility, will always confirm the facility manager's claim that it is the project creating a momentary dip in facility productivity.

Now the really insidious part of the Project Junkie disease begins. When most projects tend to stretch their timelines, and the nine months turn into twelve, somewhere around the 80% completion part of the timetable, the facility manager will dream up and pitch the next major project: "You know the total re-layout is going to produce a 12% increase in productivity, so that's just about in the bag. But what will really cause this facility to zoom is the installation of VNA [very narrow aisle], and I have a quote showing how we can get a six-month ROI if we install VNA in our Building #3. This is a no-brainer!"

Some victims of the Project Junkie disease have managed to go from one major project to another for years, all the time shielding themselves from their boss's productivity expectations. Granted, these are severe cases — true Project Junkies — but there's a little bit of this malady in all of us. As a consequence, the tracking systems for incentive plans, process improvements, or engineering design upgrades need to take this proclivity into consideration.

Project Junkie Antidote

There is a clear-cut way for the corporate sponsor to monitor the amount of gainshares, then see if the facility manager turns the incentives into labor savings for the company.

PRODUCTIVITY RULE #44

Oversight is required by the corporate sponsor. Project Junkies can be mitigated.

Depending on the culture of your company, the corporate sponsor should manage labor savings expectations. We made the culture comment because this strategy depends on how much centralization your company can tolerate. For instance, not each and every gainshare should necessarily be turned into an hour out the door. Some of these should indeed go into projects that can produce savings in the future, or a sustained housekeeping drive, increased inventory control, etc.

But let's take a look at the monthly chart below.

FACILITY #3	Monthly Gainshares	Hours Saved	$ Saved
REPO	$1,120.00	448	$7,696.64
SHIPPING	$520.00	208	$3,573.44
RECEIVING	$680.00	272	$4,672.96
ORDERFILLING	$2,440.00	896	$15,393.28
OTHER	$1,000.00	400	$6,872.00
OFFICE	$720.00	288	$4,947.84
STOCKING	$600.00	240	$4,123.20
TOTALS:	$7,080.00	2,752	$47,279.36
The gainsharing plan generates total company savings of $40,199.36 ($47,279.36 – $7,080.00).			

When the various classifications are totaled up from this facility's monthly Simplified Gainsharing payouts, you see that 2,752 hours were saved this month.

If this were a four-week month, you would expect an FTE would work 160 hours, and in its most elementary sense, the facility saved a potential 17.2 people this month. While it's doubtful the facility allowed no projects or ancillary work this month, there should have been considerable labor savings to the company. As such, it's up to the corporate sponsor to determine a fair amount of FTE reduction to this facility's workforce; exactly how much is dependent on how much autonomy is allowed the facility managers, and how well this particular facility is doing on its budgets.

Even so, if this facility ran 200 FTEs on average at the beginning of a Simplified Gainsharing installation, it would be reasonable to see a new average in the 190 range, dependent on the project authorizations for this facility.

Salaried Sliding Scales

Clearly there's a potential landmine for corporate headquarters when incentive plans begin to generate an excess in hours beyond what the facility needs to process the day's work.

Corporate may not see the financial synergies it expects from all the gainshares paid out if these "extra" hours are poured into special projects.

What's a company to do?

First, the corporate sponsor needs to create tracking mechanisms, similar to those provided in Chapter 1, but more fleshed out and tailored to the company's specific needs. There should be a clear expectation regarding the relationship between gainshares paid and labor hours saved. This relationship should be clearly telegraphed to the facility managers as a road map to improved labor ratios. However, it should be just that — a road map — rather than a draconian approach from corporate to squeeze every possible hour out of a facility.

PRODUCTIVITY RULE #45

Avoid special project landmines. Create salaried incentive systems that drive hours out of the facility.

But there's a better way to drive hours out of a facility's operating statement when Simplified Gainsharing takes hold.

We suggest taking the same approach with the managers and supervisors as you did with the blue-collar workforce when you instituted Simplified Gainsharing. Structure their bonus programs based on a sliding scale with no caps, and shorten the payout periods from annual to monthly.

Indeed, all the same components are applicable to salaried employees, even though this approach has rarely been applied to this group.

That's the idea in a nutshell. You need to create an incentive device that will motivate the managers and supervisors of a facility to automatically fight their natural impulses for creating more projects and instead to automatically drive labor hours out of the facility. Such an incentive plan is necessary if the company is going to achieve full financial benefits from the gainshares that it pays out.

Let's look at the components of such a managerial and supervisory bonus plan.

Single measurement

Select a single productivity measurement that has the endorsement of all the facility managers in your network. We favor some type of formula where the standard throughput number is determined by dividing volume in plus volume out plus transfer and debt volumes by hours actually worked in the facility (which excludes vacations and holiday hours) per month. The benefit of a throughput metric is that it measures all the major activities of a distribution center, both inbound and outbound, in contrast to lines per employee or sales per employee, which are both outbound measurements.

$$\frac{\text{(Volume In)} + \text{(Volume Out)} + \text{(Transfer and Debit Volumes)}}{\text{Hours Worked in Facility Excluding Vacation and Holiday Hours}} = \text{Throughput per Hour}$$

Sliding scales, no caps

We recommend that — just like the blue-collar sliding scales — you design a target throughput number for the facility where you pay out a bonus, then up the bonus for every half a percent or a full percent above the target. And, staying in accordance with the blue-collar plan, we recommend that there are no caps on your managerial or supervisory sliding scales. Have your accountants structure what the appropriate payout should be for increases in facility productivity, but the theory is that salaried employees in the facility should receive more bonuses the higher they drive their facility's productivity. The no-cap feature of the plan will encourage the facility management to incessantly brainstorm to develop strategies for driving the facility's productivity higher and higher.

Shortened payout periods

Most salaried bonus plans pay out annually. This has been the traditional method. However, we're suggesting you break out of tradition and design a bonus plan that pays out monthly or, at worst, quarterly. Why?

We've seen a direct relationship between the frequency of payout and the degree of interest that can be maintained in an incentive plan. With blue-collar workers, the ideal would be to reward the superlative performance of one day with a payout the next day. That would be the ideal — but not very realistic. A weekly payout would be better — but again, not easily achievable in most companies. That's why we recommend monthly payouts in Simplified Gainsharing.

PRODUCTIVITY RULE #46

Excitement levels in a facility will be greatly enhanced when all employees — both hourly and salaried — are put on similar payout periods.

With salaried employees, the dynamics are the same, even though they're accustomed to annual bonus payouts. But you can dramatically increase the excitement level in your supervisors and managers by changing the payout periods to monthly. Of course, the payouts themselves would be reduced accordingly (by one twelfth), but that does not reduce the excitement or achievement level in your salaried employees. Instead, it increases their levels and adds impetus to your Simplified Gainsharing efforts in the facility. They quickly pick up on the performance/reward relationship, and the whole facility — blue-collar and salaried employees — forges ahead with productivity improvements.

A variation of this recommendation would be to pay out half of a monthly bonus and hold back the other half as an annual lump sum based on the overall annual performance of the facility. This smoothes out some of the monthly anomalies that may occur in those facilities where throughput receives a lift from abnormally increased inbound or sales.

To complete our examination of a suggested salaried incentive plan:

Variable by facility

Not all facilities in your network should have the same starting points or goals in your salaried incentive plans. We suggest breaking your facilities into thirds, based on a productivity ranking of your network. For instance, take the highest one third of your facilities and give them the highest throughput goals while also giving them the highest monthly payouts. Decrease both the goals and the payouts when structuring the middle and bottom one thirds of your facilities.

PRODUCTIVITY RULE #47

The same components that ignite your blue-collar workers will also inspire your salaried employees.

The highest productivity facilities are the ones that are going to pull your whole network higher. Recognizing this, you should be sensitive to designing incentive programs that can ignite the imaginations of the salaried employees within these facilities. For example, if the other facilities are paid more for each percent gained on their sliding scales, then the highest facilities should be paid for each one-half percent on the sliding scales.

Why do this? One reason is that each facility should be incentivized primarily based on its own performance. But a better reason is to recognize the fact that it's easier to raise the productivity 20% in your lowest performing facility than it is to raise the productivity of your highest performing facility by 20%. In short, it's a lot more difficult to move a facility upward when all the fat has already been wrung out. As such, the highest performing facilities have often been penalized in salaried incentive plans when they're given the same percentage increase goals as all the other facilities.

Employees at the top facilities will see this as fair and actually a relief from being treated the same as those in the lowest performing facilities. And whenever the participants in your incentive plan think the plan is very fair, you're already miles ahead in your quest for success.

Chapter 10
The Audacious Goal

To reach the goal of doubling network productivity, you need to set audacious goals at the facility level. And that means you need to begin by figuring out how to hyper-motivate your best facility manager.

Consider again that anomaly of rankings — the 20% rule. We've already discussed the banshees and zombies that can be found in any employee group. In the managerial ranks, this is also usually true, only to a lesser degree. The zombies don't long survive the Darwinian pursuit of corporate profit, so you will find few of them in groups of 20 managers. But even among managers, you'll likely find a couple at the bottom end, ready to be pruned or transformed.

Start with the banshee managers. You need to get them to transcend their own goals. Most banshee managers have one basic pursuit — to be at the top of the rankings. Usually they are riveted on numbers that demonstrate their own number one position, and usually they are thinking about a point of achievement 10% or 15% beyond the top range in the company's various measurements.

As an aside, it's interesting to note that nearly every facility manager will draw attention to the one measurement in which their facility is doing well. Some managers are quite inventive in working the P&Ls to dig out arcane numbers to demonstrate that their facility is actually doing pretty well, in spite of all the unique albatrosses they carry on their shoulders. This is why the corporate sponsor, and the corporation itself, should focus on one or two overarching measurements that can quickly define the success of a facility when measured against the other facilities.

But back to the banshee managers: Pick out your best manager, the best facility, or one of the best in whom you have the most faith in executing the managerial techniques you're going to bring to the facility. Go to the facility and meet with the manager and the senior staff of the facility — no more than four people should be in your audience. Walk to the front of the room and write on the white board or a flip chart a single, solitary, lonely number.

The figure you're going to write — in big, bold numbers — represents a 35% increase in productivity above the top number the facility has ever averaged in a single month. Be brave, be audacious.

If you picked the right facility, you should get a response of good-natured laughter, tinged with a certain awe for the goal. After all, these are people who understand the thrill of the big achievement.

So far you're doing great, and you're off to a good start: You have them reacting to your initial goal.

Stay with it. "Okay, I can see you think this is a little bit of a stretch goal. But just bear in mind, I wouldn't have the nerve to stand in front of any other facility management team in the network and write such a number on the board. This is the only place I would even think to write something like this."

PRODUCTIVITY RULE #48

Begin your Audacious Goal campaign with a banshee manager from one of your best facilities.

When the chuckling finally begins to abate, and they're beginning to get the idea you seriously want them to consider this stretch goal, ask them something like, "What if someone held a gun to your head? What if someone actually threatened to end your life unless you came up with a way to hit a 30% increase? Would something like that compel you to passionately consider ways to hit this goal? Would it get you to brainstorm until you figured out a way to do it? Because the fact of the matter is: our competitors figuratively have guns to our corporate head, and our financial lives are in jeopardy every day."

At any rate, this is the group you have to engage and then lead through brainstorming sessions until you come up with a workable plan to hit the big number. By a workable plan we mean a plan that this operating team of managers has helped create and has expressed faith in their ability to make it work. You might have to conduct numerous sessions with them; you might have to make return visits, but if you are tenacious and hang in there with this group of managers, they will develop a road map toward your 35% number. We have never seen a team of the best managers in the best facility fail to create such a plan.

Indeed, the failure to achieve audacious goals always lies with the bosses of banshees who never have the audacity to dream big, who never have the audacity to walk to a white board in front of banshee managers and write a big, bold number on it.

Once the banshee facility has mapped out a plan on how to achieve 35% above the best productivity number ever recorded by your network, you'll need to do a few things.

First, allow them to run a few months with their plan. The prime directive of the corporate sponsor is to allow the banshees to fly. You might have phone conferences with them occasionally, and you should always be on the lookout to give them any assistance they need, or always be ready to dream up ways to remove any impediment from their performance; but the best counsel is to allow the banshees of this first facility to run. Listen closely to what they are saying, but the attainment of this goal, this achievement of the 35%, needs to be their own achievement.

It doesn't hurt to have weekly phone conferences, or to visit now and then, as long as too much attention doesn't clip the banshees' wings. Indeed, it's a fine line between allowing the banshees to fly and badgering them to hit a 35% productivity increase. However, the banshee management team needs to know their quest is not only for the greater glory of their own facility; they also need to understand they will be providing leadership to the whole network. They are a laboratory, and are developing methods and best practices that you will be able to export to the other facilities in the network. The banshees will be modeling how to achieve the big numbers, and you can use their facility to lead the whole network toward greater profitability.

This is exactly what a banshee wants to hear. Any banshee manager worth his salt will knock himself silly to demonstrate this type of leadership.

We wish we could just give you the plan to increase productivity in your best facility by 35% in less than a year. We'd sell a lot more books if this were something that can be gant-charted for all facilities. But the sad fact remains that the path to all these great increases is different for each facility. The most important part is getting your banshee facility managers to write their own plans; and that is precisely what we're charting and describing in these chapters. We clearly understand the components of greatness, but you yourself will have to fill in the actual details.

PRODUCTIVITY RULE #49

Banshee managers never fail to plan out and achieve audacious goals. Rather, the bosses of banshees fail to challenge them to hit gigantic goals.

The components for establishing audacious goals and doubling network productivity are relatively simple.

Component #1. Have a good blue-collar productivity/incentive plan installed in all facilities, and make sure all your facility managers are hitting on all cylinders in administering it. This plan should be based on individual performance and sliding scales with no caps. It will probably come as no surprise that we recommend this plan be Simplified Gainsharing. This will dramatically change the complexion of how productivity levels are viewed by the employees in your facilities.

Component #2. Have a good salaried incentive plan installed in all your facilities, one based on sliding scales with no caps, so the higher the management and supervisory teams drive the facility's productivity, the more bonuses they make. This will dramatically change the complexion of how productivity levels are viewed by the managers in your company.

Component #3. After these two components have been up and running for six to twelve months, choose the facility with the best productivity record, which hopefully also contains your best management and supervisory team, and hold a meeting with the top three or four managers in that facility. Write an audacious productivity number on the whiteboard.

Component #4. Get the managers of this first facility comfortable and then excited about your audacious goal. Help them brainstorm and write a plan to achieve this number within six months. Give them enough room to fly, but be on the lookout to remove any impediment to their plan.

Component #5. Once your original facility is halfway toward its goal, and has now taken a big move upward from what had been the top of your performance rankings, it's time to get other managers in your network engaged in their own audacious goals. Once it becomes clear that one facility is well on its way to reaching an audacious goal, you can start talking to other facility managers about how to attain audacious numbers. However, you'll first have to contend with the Seven Stages of Managerial Death, which are described in the following chapter.

PRODUCTIVITY RULE #50

Once the banshee facility manager has planned out the 35% increase, remove all possible road-blocks while giving him enough space to fly.

Component #6. Understand the Seven Stages and nurse all your facility managers through them.

Component #7. Understand the traits of your company's banshee managers, then disseminate these traits throughout all your facilities and managers. Many discussions of these banshee manager topics will follow the chapter on the Seven Stages.

Component #8 Stay focused on a 100% productivity increase in the network over the next five years. Repeat components three through eight as needed, until you reach your own audacious goal of doubling network productivity.

Chapter 11
The Seven Stages
Of Managerial Death

The corporate sponsor of Simplified Gainsharing who chooses the audacious goal will see an odd phenomenon when propagating this goal and instilling it in facility managers in the network.

We call the phenomenon, respectfully, the Seven Stages of Managerial Death. Not that a discussion of goal setting leads inevitably toward corporate or career death — it doesn't, of course — but when managers first hear about the audacious goal, they respond in a manner that appears to mimic the seven stages of death. The corporate sponsor who understands this phenomenon will take great pains to lead the facility managers through the first seven stages (avoiding the eighth stage — death — by the way).

Facility managers shouldn't be expected to instantly — or even quickly — accept the audacious goal. Instead, the corporate sponsor will need to be prepared to spend as much time as needed (and this time element will probably be different for each individual facility manager) to bring all the facility managers through the six stages and end with acceptance of the goal. The better the corporate sponsor understands this phenomenon, the better chance the company will have of hitting the audacious goal. For, in the end, no facility manager can really achieve a goal unless they first believe in its possibility and can visualize the steps needed to make the numbers.

This whole discussion of the Seven Stages concept might appear counterintuitive given the image of the hard-charging facility manager who always maintains the most positive of attitudes. But it occurs in many forms and with great rapidity. Remember, it was Carl Jung who once said, "We cannot change anything until we accept it."

The seven stages will begin as soon as you introduce the audacious goal, although each individual manager moves through the stages in their own unique way, some taking weeks or even months. They go something like this:

Denial

We can't hit this goal, the manager thinks. No facility has ever achieved a number like this. Are you crazy? This is impossible. You're asking for something beyond the bounds of managerial possibility. It can't be done. You want us to go where no man has gone before!

Bargaining

Can't we wait until all our projects are done? At least then we would have a shot at it. You don't want us to push so hard that we melt down the facility, do you?

Disbelief

We just don't see how this can be done. How can a facility really rise to such a level? How can you run a facility with 30% less employees and get the same business done? You can't run a facility for free, you know.

PRODUCTIVITY RULE #51

The acceptance of an audacious goal requires a process similar to the seven stages of death. Wise corporate sponsors take a lot of pains to nurse all the facility managers through this process.

Anger

This is outrageous! How can you ask us to do the impossible? You're telling us to jeopardize the smooth functioning of our facilities. If we cut out all these FTEs, our facilities will go into meltdown. You'll ruin the whole company! And what about our careers? You're really asking us to put our careers on the line.

Guilt

Okay, maybe we are looking at it as the glass is half-full. But do we really want to lay off all these employees? We don't know if that's really fair. However, we do want to be head and shoulders above the competition — don't get us wrong — it's just we're not sure we can do this without knocking over the apple cart.

Depression

We just don't know why the company thinks that every year we can stretch so far beyond the attainable budgets. If they want us to hit these numbers, why don't they just do the budgets for us instead of making us go through the formality of creating a budget? Maybe we're just not smart enough.

Acceptance

Okay, okay, maybe we've whined enough. If this is the challenge the company has given us, well then, let's take a good run at it. Each of us has done more difficult things in the past. Besides, it's going to give the company the competitive edge it needs to come out on top. And we can play a big part in the company's success. We can demonstrate that with the right moxie, people can hit the big audacious goals. Let's take a shot at it!

We must admit this process is a phenomenon, and we really can't explain why highly successful facility managers need to go through a reasoning process so similar to the seven stages of death, but we see it time and time again. It's as though it's an essential component of our human nature that dictates the bigger the achievement, the more pronounced become the initial stages of the logic that gets our minds from first hearing the audacious goal, to conceiving the possibility, to at last accepting the idea that this number can indeed be achieved. Rarely does any manager accept the audacious goal on first hearing. As such, the wise corporate sponsor will recognize the process, and nurse along all the facility managers at their own pace, until they all come out the other end and accept the audacious goal.

And the wise corporate sponsor will also need to possess a clear understanding of the managerial traits of the company's own banshee managers.

Chapter 12
Managerial Best Practices — Benchmarking Your Own Network

What are the best managerial traits of your own banshee managers? Benchmarking and Best Practices are techniques that gain instant recognition and approval in managerial ranks, yet there is a similar practice that can bring even bigger results — Managerial Best Practices. How do the best managers manage? What do they do that's different to motivate their own workforces?

Allow us to suggest an interesting exercise: Bring your three best facility managers together for a two-day brainstorming session in order to determine the common denominators in their management practices. You might want to engage the services of a consultant or a professional brainstormer who can conduct the session as an objective third party, but it's not essential. If you want to conduct the meetings yourself, such brainstorming is not particularly difficult.

PRODUCTIVITY RULE #52

Conduct a brainstorming session with your best managers to discover the common denominators of success in your own network. Most likely you'll discover the majority of them are managerial behaviors.

We believe what you'll discover is a one-third/two-thirds split in the nature of the common denominators — the practices these three managers think are important factors in achieving their superlative numbers. We think you'll find that approximately one third will be operating practices or nuts-and-bolts process techniques and procedures that any other manager can readily adopt to uptick a facility. Good stuff. But what is even more interesting to us is how the other two thirds of what your own best managers will relate most likely falls under the category of managerial behaviors.

The behaviors sound easy to duplicate, but the appearance of ease is deceptive. In the business of the workday and daily production, most managers gravitate toward quantifiable fixes, the operating nuts and bolts, rather than embracing the goalsetting or motivational side of the management game. It's somewhat the same phenomenon that makes Simplified Gainsharing more successful under most managers than the participative management of the original gainsharing techniques. We shouldn't necessarily expect all our managers to be HR gurus.

However, when managers contemplate the managerial practices brought up by the best managers of a network as common denominators of their success, there are many topics that can indeed be adapted and adopted. As such, we're going to examine those topics that bubble up as common denominators among top managers.

We think you'll agree that none of what follows is brain surgery, and can indeed be duplicated as managerial best practices.

Banshee Managers — the Audacious Goal

The first common denominator among the managers of the best facilities is a commitment to an audacious goal.

Scratch a great manager, and the first thing you'll find is a manager who self-motivates in the selection of a great goal for the facility. These managers — on their own — will select a goal they think will propel them beyond all the other facilities in the network, and any other facilities owned by the competition.

PRODUCTIVITY RULE #53

Banshee managers ultimately convince their subordinates to commit to the audacious goal. Banshee managers create banshee supervisors.

After they select an audacious goal, they motivate and rally their management team and supervisory staff to commit to the goal. This takes persuasion, this takes persistence, this takes numerous speeches and communications to everyone in the facility — in short, this takes leadership. Also, the great managers have the courage to not only enunciate their goals to all the people in their own facilities, they also have the courage to publicly state their audacious goal to the other managers in the network. You can't be great by coming in the back door.

Walk into a great manager's facility, and shortly you'll be bombarded with messages concerning the audacious goal. You'll see signs and banners describing the big number and where the facility stands in achieving it. Talk to a supervisor and you'll hear the audacious number come up in conversation. Ask an employee what the facility manager wants to achieve, and regardless of the employees' attitude, you'll hear the goal. And most people in the facility can describe why the attainment of the goal is important — it's not just a personal goal of the facility manager, it's important for the financial health of the company and, as such, is important for preserving the good employment of everyone in the facility.

The great manager incessantly drives the audacious goal every single day, thinking of new and novel ways to get the message across. All managers and supervisors in the facility come to believe in the great manager's goal. All of them rally to the great manager's vision. Those who don't will eventually leave.

A way to prove this last theory is to look at what happens when the company transfers a great manager to a facility that's in trouble. The great manager, being a banshee, will choose an audacious goal for the facility. However, a facility under stress, and at the bottom of the network rankings, is generally filled with managers and supervisors who do not have positive visions for the future performance of the facility. Trust that the great manager will within a few years bring that facility to the top. However, few of the original supervisors will remain on the staff, simply because few of them will buy into the great manager's vision and will either leave or be asked to leave. In their place will be people who readily buy into the audacious goal.

Great managers require everyone on their staffs to commit to the audacious goal — it's the only way for the facility to achieve excellence.

Banshee Managers — Brainstorming

The second common denominator among managers of the best facilities as it concerns managerial practices is constant brainstorming with their staffs to hit the audacious goal.

Brainstorming is a wonderful device to find ways to reach the audacious goal; however, the banshee manager must first move the management team and the supervisory staff through the Seven Stages of Managerial Death and help them arrive at Acceptance. Only when the team arrives at Acceptance can it truly begin to brainstorm on ideas that will get the facility to the heights of the audacious goal.

PRODUCTIVITY RULE #54

One brainstorming session does not a great achievement make. Brainstorm incessantly.

The trick to brainstorming is to do it incessantly. One brainstorming session does not a great achievement make. It takes many sessions. You never know when the great idea is going to surface, but you must have faith that if you persevere in the brainstorming sessions, valuable ideas will indeed bubble up.

How do you keep the brainstorming sessions fresh? A change of meeting rooms and change of days is always appropriate. Change the session leaders or moderators. Bring in a professional, or bring in supervisors from other facilities. Bring your brainstormers to sessions you plan after touring other facilities. Take them out to restaurant banquet rooms or to a spa or even a resort. In short, there are hundreds of ways to keep the sessions fresh. Be inventive.

To keep the excitement in the air, always have the audacious goal, in big, bold numbers, on display at all your brainstorming sessions. Continue to sell the reasonability of the audacious goal. Continue to explain it in terms of the financial health of the whole company. This is why it is of paramount importance for your facility to hit the audacious goal.

And do it incessantly. Session by session, step by step, banshee managers move their facilities toward their audacious goal. In a sense, it's not the individual ideas that are of supreme importance in achieving the goal, but instead it is the constant attention the management team pays to attaining the audacious goal.

See Appendix 6 for guidelines for conducting brainstorming sessions.

Banshee Managers — Blue-Collar Incentives

Banshee managers are also attuned to what best motivates the blue-collar workforce.

In the constant search for the better engine to drive productivity, we believe that Simplified Gainsharing hits the main buttons for greatly enhanced performance from the hourly workforce. The buttons are individualized incentives, short payout periods, sliding scales with no caps, and paying the incentives as an hourly wage.

But as much as Simplified Gainsharing is a plug & play program, it's not miraculous. We wish we could simply email it to you, and you could install it tomorrow, and then never have to worry about incentives again as your workforce doubles its productivity over the next five years or so. But banshee managers know it's not quite that easy.

PRODUCTIVITY RULE #55

Banshee managers are incessant about keeping their incentive plans sharp.

Banshee managers know that the real action in any incentive program is the action that occurs between the supervisors and the blue-collar employees. That's the firing line. Plug & play programs are relatively simple because banshee employees can tune in fast to make a lot of dough, but if you really want to rock and roll with an incentive program, the supervisors must — each and every day — trumpet its virtues to their employees.

Banshee supervisors will do this naturally, but banshee managers know that, try as they might, their departments are not populated entirely by banshee supervisors.

The solution is for banshee managers to daily make certain that their incentive program is fine-tuned and firing on all cylinders. They champion the program within their own facilities as ardently as the corporate sponsor champions the program in the network. It's fairly simple in the minds of banshee managers — if you're going to hit the audacious goal, you must drive a significant amount of FTEs out of the workforce, and the simplest way to do this is to constantly and incessantly work your incentive plan.

All incentive plans grow whiskers if they are not vigilantly maintained by the facility manager, so banshee managers are religious in their maintenance and are constantly on the lookout for new ways to trumpet their program to both their supervisors and the workforce.

This is where the action is.

Banshee Managers — Tracking Hours

Banshee managers track every hour in the facility.

This might sound obsessive, but . . . well, there are no buts. It is indeed obsessive. If you aspire to be a banshee manager and hit the audacious goal, then you must be obsessive about each and every hour spent inside your facility.

Now wait just one minute! We've never met a facility manager who didn't track hours spent in their facility. Isn't this part of the job? Shipping, receiving, inbound and outbound, production and non-production, hours per throughput — it's all there on their spreadsheets.

But this is really just accumulating hours, it's not tracking every hour.

Banshee managers instruct their supervisors to track each and every hour that is spent in their department by the day. They want each supervisor to know precisely how each employee in their department spends every single hour, every single day. Now that's obsessive — but there's even more.

Banshee managers then hold daily meetings during which supervisors report precisely how many hours were spent in their departments the previous day. Banshee managers want to know their supervisors have a firm understanding where all the hours are going and why they're going there. And they want them to have opinions on how these hours can be reduced while still getting the work done.

The best way for supervisors to become and stay obsessive on hour tracking is for banshee managers to figure out a way to calculate how the hours in each supervisors' department relate to the audacious goal. This will require the banshee manager to calculate the audacious goal on each day's production, and then divide it fairly among the various departments based on how many FTEs each supervisor has in the work group.

PRODUCTIVITY RULE #56

Track every single hour spent by every single employee every single day. Track it by supervisor. Daily managerial analysis of hours spent — conducted in supervisor meetings — will automatically decrease FTEs.

Once these calculation methods are achieved, a number of interesting things will become readily apparent. The first is the distinction between banshee supervisors and average supervisors. The banshee supervisors will surge forward in their competition to achieve the audacious goal in their own departments — their successes can be used to help and motivate the other supervisors. The second occurrence is that the very tracking of each and every hour per supervisor will in itself lead toward a reduction of hours used. As supervisors have to report on where they spend each and every hour, they will automatically become more thrifty in the use of those hours. As they report daily to the facility manager, the supervisors' departmental productivity improves because they come to understand more and more their part in achieving the audacious goal.

As the banshee supervisors become successful and share their successes with the other supervisors, this daily analysis of hours spent becomes one of the most significant tools in decreasing the amount of FTEs in the facility. Each morning, the supervisory staff and facility manager should analyze the hours used yesterday by every department — each success and failure of hour expenditure and how it relates to the facility's audacious goal — and then use this analysis to plan the existing day. Doing it this way, the supervisory staff will become adept at teamwork and sharing hours, and also adept at positioning the best workers in the best jobs to save hours.

The attainment of the audacious goal grows closer and closer.

Banshee Managers — Create Other Banshee Managers

Banshee managers breed like crazy — figuratively, that is.

Banshee managers understand all the components of their managerial styles and can communicate them, so it's natural for them to teach them to supervisors on their staffs.

They tell their supervisors that the first step to becoming a banshee manager is to select an audacious goal for their supervisory duties. How do you do this? They need to be aware of all the other similar departments in the network and the measurements involved in ranking these departments. Each supervisor relates to these rankings — they are either in first place, or they aren't.

The selection of the audacious goal then becomes quite simple: If the supervisor is number one in the network, then the audacious goal should be 30% above their current numbers. If the supervisor is not number one in the network, then the audacious goal should be around 10% above the best department in the entire network.

Next, the banshee manager takes the supervisors through the Seven Stages of Managerial Death, allowing them to work out all the denial and depression and anger, eventually arriving at acceptance of the audacious goal. This step may take a few weeks — it's much better to know the supervisor totally accepts the audacious goal, and is not simply giving lip service to it. The banshee manager will take pains to nurse this particular step along to fulfillment.

Now, how does the supervisor achieve the audacious goal? As banshee managers know, there are basically two main ways to do it, and both need to be done concurrently — they are brainstorming and Daily Touching (communicating face-to-face daily about goals and status).

Once the supervisor selects and accepts the audacious goal, he will become evangelistic in the pursuit of it, and will engage all the banshees in the department in the attainment of the audacious goal. Their enthusiasm will become infectious. They will incessantly brainstorm within their departments, just as they will incessantly communicate with their employees each day regarding the employees' own audacious goals.

In this manner, banshee managers turn everyone on their facility's staff into other banshee managers or banshee supervisors. Inevitably, the facility itself rises to produce banshee numbers. However, we should point out that all is not roses with this technique of banshee managers. Not every supervisor or manager in the facility will be able to make the journey through the seven stages. Some will not believe in the banshee manager's vision or will not be able to embrace the audacious goal. It's sad, but Darwinian — some of these folks will need to find other jobs outside the facility if the whole facility is going to attain its goals.

Banshee Managers — Why Art Thou?

Why do some people automatically become banshee managers? Unless you have an innate ability to peer deeply into the souls of other people, you won't have a ready answer for this question. We're in the same boat, without scientific, psychological, or metaphysical proof as to why some people automatically become banshee managers.

Some people have an extraordinary amount of drive, others have a deep need to compete, still others have greater financial goals than their peers. The list is probably endless. Some people simply have a need to be number one in nearly everything they do.

One thing we've noticed: Banshee managers rarely worry about losing their own employment. They know the best way to retain their jobs with a company is to always shoot for audacious goals. Just the continual pursuit of the audacious goal in and of itself produces better numbers than one's peers. And besides, what company in its right mind would ever get rid of a banshee manager?

Lastly, the other thing we know for certain is that banshee managers are not simply lucky finds for a company. They can readily be created.

PRODUCTIVITY RULE #57

Banshee managers are not necessarily strokes of good fortune for companies . . .they can be readily duplicated.

Sound outrageous? It's not at all. Just take a look back at this chapter and tell us which parts are impossible or outrageous. In reality any of these managerial behaviors discussed in our book can be readily adopted by any manager with a desire to become a banshee manager. It's really all about desire — the knowledge is right there for the taking.

Process or Attitude?

When talking about significant productivity improvements, we're frequently asked, "Is it process or is it attitude?"

The inference is that the power of positive thinking can take a management team just so far. Don't you somewhere along the line have to change the process or make engineering improvements in order to continue to move the organization forward? You can't put all your eggs in the positive-thinking basket, can you? So is it process or attitude?

It's both. Of course you can't rely only on positive thinking to attain significant productivity gains. But one doesn't rule out the other. Besides, we're not really recommending that positive thinking will get you leaps in productivity — we're recommending that you use an effective incentive plan to get you where you want to be.

Let's examine both process and attitude. If you go with only process improvements, you will get, over the course of time, an incremental, sustainable improvement with each change. This assumes that you've been adept at avoiding all the process junkie tendencies of your facility management groups. In short, process improvement is good — both major process changes and the little process changes that are made weekly in the facilities.

But now let's flip it around: Say you don't push process changes and only go with the mental stuff, like Simplified Gainsharing. What would happen? Humbly we say we know what happens, because we've seen it time and time again. As soon as you layer in the blue-collar incentive plan coupled with a salaried plan, where both are based on sliding scales with no caps, certain behaviors abruptly occur. First, the focus on higher numbers creates a natural lift in productivity as everyone begins to eliminate the extraneous time that creeps into every job. Second, the employees and supervisors take a renewed and intense interest in the small process improvements under their own control because it accrues to their direct benefit.

Work areas become more efficient as small layout changes are quickly implemented, the pace picks up in that percentage of the workforce which is aiming at gainshares, and everyone in the facility focuses more intensely on daily productivity reports. In short, process improvements spread like wildfire.

To us the point is clear — process improvements do not automatically lead to an uptick in the attitude of your facility. But the reverse does indeed prove out when the proper (attitudinal) improvements (such as Simplified Gainsharing) lead to the proliferation of process improvements. So the answer to the question, "Is it process or attitude?" is that it's both. But if you concentrate first on the attitude and hit a home run there, all the processes will automatically improve.

Chapter 13
And Now What? Create a Fantasy Workforce

Once you've implemented Simplified Gainsharing, you see huge improvements and everyone lives happily ever after, right? Not so fast. Let's look into the future. We trust that things are going well by the time your network begins its third year of Simplified Gainsharing. Productivity is up considerably, turnover is down dramatically. Quality is improved and morale is soaring in both your salaried and blue-collar groups. You've been a big success — congratulations! But now what do you do?

One answer is to make certain you're conducting the necessary buyout audits and installing any buyouts in a manner that is satisfactory to both the employees and the company.

PRODUCTIVITY RULE #58

Sometime during the second or third year of a mature Simplified Gainsharing program, the facility will be ready for the best bold move.

But where do you go from here? It's time to add a little jolt to the program, time to re-invigorate things, isn't it? Of course it is, but let's start this discussion by examining one of your facilities. Say the workforce there is down to 100 blue-collar employees. After a solid two years of Simplified Gainsharing, the average facility should shake out something like this regarding the participation in gainshares:

11 employees are earning at 40%+ levels

14 employees are earning at 31–39% levels

18 employees are earning at 16–30% levels

30 employees are earning at 5–15% levels

25 employees are no earning gainshares

2 employees are zombies, and are near termination

Ideally what you would like to do is end up with a facility run by all banshees in the 40%+ category. But where do you find such a workforce?

What you really need is Pete the Pipe Guy.

Pete the Pipe Guy

If you check out Appendix 3 ("The Supervisor's Checklist"), you'll see that we recommend that the corporate sponsor periodically hand out $20 bills to banshee employees in the facilities. When one of the authors was in the position of corporate sponsor, he came across a phenomenal employee named Pete.

Pete worked in one of the most difficult orderfilling sections of the facility — the pipe section. His section contained about a thousand SKUs of various lengths of pipe, both metal and PVC. It used to be a three-person section, prior to Simplified Gainsharing, but now Pete was doing the work of all three orderfillers.

During a facility visit, the corporate sponsor was told about Pete, and quickly suggested that Pete would be the perfect recipient of the $20 award. The facility manager agreed, and they started downstairs to talk to Pete. On the way down to the floor, the corporate sponsor tried to imagine what Pete would look like. He pretty much decided that Pete would be a young, muscular guy, and since he was toting lengths and bundles of heavy pipe, he would actually look more like Arnold the pipe guy — "Hasta la vista, pipe!"

PRODUCTIVITY RULE #59

Nearly every facility has a Pete the Pipe Guy. Study him for a day.

Instead, the corporate sponsor found himself being introduced to an aging hippie (someone the corporate sponsor himself aspired to become one day), and went to shake hands with Pete.

But Pete was filling a pipe order, and really didn't want to stop. Reluctantly he shook hands and even smiled a little, but then took off, trying to complete his order.

The corporate sponsor speeded up to stay next to Pete, "We just wanted to say, Pete, that we sure appreciate the work you're doing."

"Thanks," said Pete. He swiftly moved to the next bin and removed a length of plastic pipe.

"No, really," the corporate sponsor said, jumping out of the way as Pete swung the pipe to his cart. "Employees like you are the backbone of the corporation."

"Kind of you," said Pete, who disappeared into the next aisle.

The corporate sponsor ran after him. "Pete, we were hoping you'd have lunch today on the company." He held out the $20 bill.

Pete snatched it. "Thanks. 'Preciate it!" He ran off — pocketing the dough — toward his next pick.

The facility manager smiled and shook his head. "Pete wastes no time!" he called to the corporate sponsor. "He's shooting for the next higher gainshare!"

The facility manager had inadvertently mentioned the secret in a nutshell — Pete wastes no time. He wasn't a super-human, he was an aging hippie. But from the first second of the day until the last, Pete the Pipe Guy wasted absolutely no time. He was totally zoned in on his mission of making the highest possible gainshare.

The corporate sponsor and the facility manager went back upstairs to the manager's office. "You know," the corporate sponsor joked, "if all your employees were like Pete, you would only need half of them." He chuckled.

"Not to mention," the facility manager grinned, "our facility productivity would double!"

Both men stopped smiling as the dawning realization descended on them. What if it were possible to turn everyone into a Pete? Every facility in the network contained one or two employees like Pete, employees who were hitting high levels of gainshares. But frankly, each facility manager in the network considered the facility to be extremely lucky just to have one of these super-banshees. Having a great employee was seen as a singular stroke of luck, as though the Lords of Logistics had bestowed a wonderful gift on the distribution center. No one in the past had ever thought about trying to turn more employees into super-banshees. Could it even be done?

PRODUCTIVITY RULE #60

Super-banshees rarely look like Olympic athletes.

The corporate sponsor's first inclination was to say, "No, it can't be done. How do you get everyone in the plant to think like Pete?"

Of course, we all have to work through the seven stages in our own ways, even corporate sponsors. Consider again the statement: "Can we get them all to think like Pete?" The real key is the word *think*. The importance of this revelation is that it requires a major shift in managerial thinking and managerial behaviors. Remember the part of the story where the corporate sponsor is walking down to the floor, expecting to see someone who looked like an Olympic body builder?

What did he find? Arnold wasn't down there. Instead a regular guy was down there. This led the corporate sponsor to take a poll of all the other facility managers, simply asking them to describe the physiques of their best employees.

What he discovered from his informal poll was that nearly all the super-banshees — both men and women — were actually very ordinary people. There were no Olympic athletics leading the network!

What does this fact mean in the brave new world of audacious goals? We think it means it's easier to achieve audacious goals if you understand what motivates super-banshees.

Chapter 14
Super-Banshee Motivations

If all the super-banshees in the network are not superhuman, why do they do it? Why do they perform their work at such a screaming level? And how can more employees come to this state of productivity?

There are probably as many motivations for super-banshees as there are super-banshees themselves. Again, we define super-banshees as employees who are at least 60% to 70% above the acceptable minimum. The famous Pete was 225% above standard, and it appeared he was always zoned in on the next level of gainshare, the next 25-cent raise. But let's examine the major motivations for super-banshees:

Wired

Some super-banshees are workers whose brains are wired to always out-perform all others. They can't help themselves. Even when they're mad at the company or mad at the world, they still out-perform all other workers. Facilities are blessed to have these people employed in their workforce.

PRODUCTIVITY RULE #61

There are myriad reasons why employees decide to become super-banshees. Supervisors need to understand them all so they can create more super-banshees.

Boredom

Super-banshees understand early on in their careers that the best way to combat the boredom of a job is to work at faster and faster speeds. Indeed, there's a direct correlation between the speed of the job performed and the speed at which time passes for the one who performs the job. The best way to prove this is to simply try the inverse — slow down your work to a crawl, and you'll quickly see that time itself slows down accordingly.

Some super-banshees are workers who are happy to work faster because it helps them pass the time more easily.

Dough

The great thing about Simplified Gainsharing is that everyone in the workforce is paid exactly, precisely, and absolutely what they think they're worth. If you're in the workforce and you think you're worth more money, it's there for the taking. Just kick it up a little and hit a higher gainshare level. Or if you think you're simply an average worker, then just do the minimum, and you'll receive the normal wages without any gainshares. In short, everyone is paid what they think they're worth.

Some super-banshees are people who have a very high opinion of what their work is worth, and as a consequence they spend their days figuring out how to hit higher and higher levels of gainshares. Over the years, as they uptick their performance little by little each month, they end up at an admirable rate of pay. The famous Pete would fall in this category.

Free Time

Many workers are not motivated at all by the opportunity to earn more money. They could care less about the dollars. But they are keenly interested in something else — more time off.

PRODUCTIVITY RULE #62

Many facility managers think it's a matter of luck when one of their employees turns into a super-banshee. But they can be created.

Free time! What better way to counteract the boredom of the job than to be physically off the job? In Appendix 4 we have a graphic that can be used to show employees how much time off they can take at each gainshare level and still take home a 40-hour check at the old standard rate of pay.

Work Ethic and Competition

Some people have a healthy dose of a good old-fashioned work ethic. They believe that when you do a job, you always do it to the best of your ability. This trait is often akin to competitive spirit, and both are frequently found in the same employee. Some super-banshees simply want to be the best worker in the facility, and they will allow no one to beat them.

Recognition

There are super-banshees who thrive on the recognition of their supervisors and managers. To them there is nothing better in their work life than to be given a productivity award, something they can take home and show their family.

But before you start publicly recognizing super-banshees, be forewarned: We've seen super-banshees who exhibit the exact opposite of this trait, and would rather be flayed alive than be called up to the podium at an assembly to accept an award.

Ambition

There are some super-banshees who are looking ahead to the rest of their careers, and they see the gainshares as a good way to publicize the fact that they are supervisory material. To them it's a clear way to show management what they are made of.

It's important that you consider all the motivations of super-banshees, because you need a lot more of them in your network or facility. In the following chapters, we're going to tell you where to find them. They might be right under your nose.

Under Our Very Eyes

Clearly there is no sole motivating factor for all super-banshees. And indeed, it's difficult to identify all the factors that drive each of us.

But what if you could clone Pete the Pipe Guy?

Imagine that. We could reduce our workforces by 50%! That would really be something! The corporate sponsor from our earlier example dwelled on this thought just long enough to come to the sad conclusion that science was not at the stage where it would allow him to clone Pete. Foiled again! Not to mention there were some moral implications to such an endeavor.

Still the corporate sponsor wasn't ready to give up on the idea. After all, if a guy like Pete could physically do it, why couldn't a lot of other workers? And why weren't they doing it right now? Simplified Gainsharing was there for everyone to make the same kind of money as Pete.

> **PRODUCTIVITY RULE #63**
>
> We can't physically clone super-banshees, but more employees can take on their attributes.

The corporate sponsor thought about the super-banshees in the other facilities. Wasn't it interesting that all the facility managers had the same take on their super-banshees? They all thought the facility was extremely fortunate to have the super-banshee employed there, as though they had hit some type of employer's lottery.

But are we simply lucky? Are we simply the poor fools who are the recipients of one or two wonderful employees? Let's take a look at how the employees break down in our distribution center:

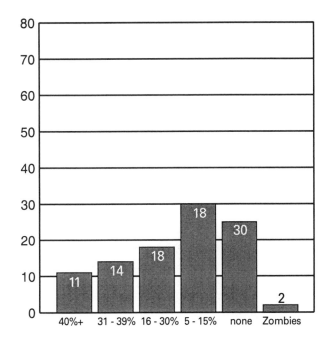

But wait just a minute. This facility had an entirely different look three years ago. The corporate sponsor realized that under management's very eyes, 75% of the employees had been taking on more and more Pete-like qualities.

The corporate sponsor called Pete's facility manager, and together they pieced together where the employees fell in the facility's productivity rankings when they started Simplified Gainsharing three years before. When Simplified Gainsharing was first implemented, the workforce looked like this:

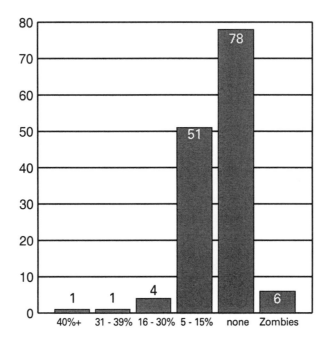

The first thing that struck them was the fact they had 141 employees in the workforce three years earlier. The next thing that struck them was the facility had actually increased its business 12% in the same time period. Hmmm . . . they were running 29% fewer employees to process 12% more business. Under their very eyes, the workforce had been collapsing itself to the more productive end of the scale. Exactly what you want a workforce to do under Simplified Gainsharing.

PRODUCTIVITY RULE #64

The secret to achieving high productivity — have a goal and waste no time at all.

Three years ago there had been only one person, Pete, in the 40%+ category, and Pete had been there only by the skin of his teeth, picking at 141% of standard. Three years later there were ten employees in the same category as Pete, although only two of them were better than 200% of minimum, and none at Pete's level.

The corporate sponsor became pretty darn excited looking at these two graphs. To his eyes the graphs emphatically answered the question of whether more Petes could be created. Clearly many of the employees themselves were headed in Pete's direction.

The corporate sponsor wondered if the process could be accelerated.

Core Ingredients

The challenge for the corporate sponsor was clear, and easy to define: How could he create more Petes?

What were the real core ingredients behind Pete's success? Certainly you could rule out superhuman physical capabilities. Not that Pete was a physical slouch — he wasn't. But he wasn't an Olympic athlete either.

So what are the core ingredients? The corporate sponsor decided to list them on paper, and after thinking it through for some time, was astounded to realize something about Pete's core ingredients: There were really just two of them. First, Pete was keenly focused on a goal. Right now it was to make $20 an hour; but before this, it had been $19 an hour, and before that $18 an hour, etc. Pete had ratcheted himself up over the past three years, dialing up a new goal each time he attained the previous goal.

PRODUCTIVITY RULE #65

The core ingredients of super-banshees are they set goals, constantly moving the bar upwards, and they're completely zoned in on their work.

Pete's second core ingredient was simply that he wasted no time at all during the day. This was his main secret, and the one that counteracted the need to be an Olympic athlete when attempting to double a standard. But Pete didn't just keep himself busy during the day. No, it went beyond that. Pete obsessively filled each minute to the max with productivity, not stopping for any reason at all. You might recall how the corporate sponsor wanted to award Pete $20, and nearly had to chase him across the whole department. Pete wasn't being rude, not at all. Pete was simply used to filling each minute to the max, and this philosophy had simply become a way of life for him. He wouldn't stop for anything or anyone.

So there it was in a nutshell — have a goal and waste no time at all.

It sounded too easy to be true. Deceptively easy. For while it might be easy to boil Pete's performance down to just two main ingredients, the difficult part was to figure out how to instill these two things in the minds of more employees in the workforce. Indeed, there's a big difference between knowing what to do, and getting other employees to embrace and implement this knowledge. And there was the rub.

The corporate sponsor realized his supervisors couldn't just go up to their employees and say, "Waste no time," and have all the employees immediately embrace this work habit. In reality, what would happen is that every employee in the facility would say something like, "What do you mean? I don't waste any time now. Why do you think I have time to waste during the workday? Are you trying to insult me?"

The corporate sponsor would have to dig a lot deeper than this.

Chapter 15
Mentoring a Fantasy Workforce

Initially it appeared to be quite the conundrum — the corporate sponsor knew the two core ingredients to Pete's success, but he couldn't easily pass the information on to the employees. They really had to conclude these things themselves.

So how do you get the message across to employees in such a manner that they will readily embrace it? And how do you identify the employees to target for the message? You can't just tell employees to focus on an audacious goal, then expect them all to say, "Oh yeah, why didn't we ever think of that? We'll snap right to it!" They're more likely to say, "40%! We'll never be able to improve by another 40%."

Such instant denial has a familiar ring to it. Isn't it just like the Seven Stages of Managerial Death? Then the corporate sponsor realized the Seven Stages don't only strike the managers, they strike everyone — employees, supervisors, managers, even corporate sponsors.

PRODUCTIVITY RULE #66

To attain the ultimate audacious goal, the Seven Stages theory needs to be applied to everyone in the network.

Let's start from the top — the ultimate audacious goal was to double the productivity of a network in five to seven years. A wonderful goal, but the first time the corporate sponsor heard it, he went right into denial. How does the network productivity double simply by managing the managers better? Of course the corporate sponsor was a fanatical positive thinker, and it wasn't long before he arrived at acceptance.

Once there, he spent the next couple of years dealing with all the seven-stage behaviors of the facility managers in the network. Twenty managers times seven stages equaled 140 stages he had to manage through.

Pretty time consuming, but it had paid off. The network productivity had increased 68% since they had started out on this mission. He was now pondering how to get that last 32%.

But if the time had come to apply the seven stages to the blue-collar employees, that meant seven stages times 3,000 employees across the network — 21,000 stages! How could he possibly manage through a task like that?

Fantasy Workforce

The corporate sponsor realized that 21,000 stages couldn't possibly be handled by one person.

Facility managers and supervisory staffs would have to be engaged. And even if the salaried crew were mobilized and had the time to spend on this new management task, they still couldn't reach out to all 3,000 employees if the idea was to properly manage someone through the seven stages. The idea would have to be refined, and it wouldn't hurt to incentivize them to conduct these new supervisory behaviors.

This was the birth of the Fantasy Workforce.

The steps involved in implementing a Fantasy Workforce program are relatively simple. Of course, it should only be implemented in a facility with a mature Simplified Gainsharing program.

Step 1: Selecting participants

Each supervisor in the facility picks out four or five employees that can be signed up to participate in an intensive mentoring program.

Actually, this particular process is how Fantasy Workforce received, and eventually lost, its wistful name. A workforce comprising all Pete the Pipe Guys would indeed be a fantasy, but the name itself came from the selection process being similar to Fantasy Football.

So why did we change the name from "Fantasy Workforce" to "Mentoring"?

PRODUCTIVITY RULE #67

Fantasy Workforce can be used to attain the final increases needed to achieve the ultimate audacious goal.

The supervisors at some of the initial facilities where we implemented Fantasy Workforce suggested this picking and trading of employees might be a tad demeaning to the workers, or might be seen as horse-trading.

While we could see their point, we thought it could be rolled out as Fantasy Workforce with the proper enthusiasm, or with the right explanations and humor. We thought it wouldn't be a bad thing at all for the employees to think of themselves as athletes or free agents. In fact, some facilities had a lot of fun with it.

But we didn't force the name. In the world of Simplified Gainsharing, the full participation of a facility's supervisory staff is always one of the most important ingredients. Over the course of the years while rolling out Simplified Gainsharing programs, we have learned that it's better to modify the rules to embrace the subculture of a facility than it is to jam rules down the throats of managers, supervisors, or employees. So as Fantasy Workforce evolved, we've gravitated more and more toward calling it Mentoring. But we think anyone would admit that "Fantasy Workforce" makes a heck of a lot better title! And if you think that Fantasy Workforce would work in your facility, we encourage you to use the term.

In our real-world example, supervisors of the beta facility met to choose four employees for each to mentor. The goal was for the supervisors to see if they could change the work behaviors of four employees to mimic the two main characteristics of super-banshees. The first thing they did was establish the rules of selection. There were eight supervisors and a workforce of 98 blue-collar employees.

Rule one: Each supervisor picked one employee with whom he thought he had a good relationship, an already established rapport so they could quickly connect. They went around the room, until each supervisor had picked four employees.

> **PRODUCTIVITY RULE #68**
>
> **Supervisors should choose employees whom they have the best chance of motivating.**

Rule two: Employees could be picked out of department, meaning the selected employee didn't have to be currently working in the choosing supervisor's department. The thinking behind this was since supervisors had rotated over the years through various departments in the facility, they had formed relationships with many of the employees. It was well known that some employees responded better to certain supervisors; in fact, each supervisor knew which employee was easiest for them to motivate.

On the other hand, the picks could also be chosen entirely from within the supervisor's own department.

Rule three: After the selection process was completed, the supervisors were allowed to trade players or employees, so certain deals were brokered as each supervisor created the strongest team possible.

Step 2: Getting employee participation

In the second step, the supervisor approaches the selected employees one at a time, to see if they are interested in participating in the mentoring process.

In most cases, the approach goes something like this: The supervisor walks up to the employee on the floor, using the opening question, "How would like to work with me over the course of the next few months to see if we can figure out how to get you a $2 an hour raise on gainshares?"

Ninety percent of employees approached with this proposition will be willing to sign up for a mentoring program that could potentially earn them a raise of this magnitude. But the supervisor needs to know the targeted employee also. Not all employees are motivated by more money. Some are better motivated by free time. An alternative approach might be, "What would you say about jumping on a program that could get you an extra six to eight hours of paid time off each week?"

Most employees approached with one of the two above methods will respond favorably. Still, there will be other employees who will require other motivations to participate in such an intense mentoring program. Have supervisors read through the list of super-banshee motivations before their selection process.

The approach is easy. The sign-up is easy. But the next question from the approached employee might be the toughest one a supervisor is ever asked to handle.

We guarantee all employees who bite on the $2 raise idea will immediately ask, "What do I have to do to get the $2 raise?" (Or, "What will I have to do to get the extra time off?")

The answer, of course, depends on how you've established your sliding scales. But in most cases, it will require an approximately 40% increase in the employee's current productivity.

"You want me to increase my production 40%! Are you nuts?"

PRODUCTIVITY RULE #69

Supervisors need to be prepared to handle the initial denial.

The Seven Stages process starts immediately, as soon as the person hears the audacious goal.

Supervisors need to be prepared with the antidote, the right persuasive medicine to cause the employee to start thinking like a superbanshee. They can't just simply say, "Hey, get a life. All you need is a big goal, and then make up your mind to waste absolutely no time at all during the work day." Wouldn't it be wonderful if it were that easy?

Supervisors need to understand the Seven Stages and be ready to counteract Denial. The employee might be somewhat offended: "Don't you think I'm busting my hump enough right now? I'm going full tilt! How could I ever get another 40%? You gotta be nuts!"

Supervisors should be agreeable. "You're right. I certainly don't think you're slacking off any at all. You're one of the best employees in the joint. I'm just saying that I believe that if you and I put our minds to it, there has to be ways for us to come up with ideas that can get you to the 40% increase. I just think it's worth $2 an hour for us to spend some time together each day."

Additional fodder for the fight for the hearts and minds of potential super-banshees:

• "I've heard about employees in other facilities who are making $5 and $6 more per hour on gainshares. They can't be smarter than the two of us. I just thought we ought to take a crack at the big money."

• "You've been working in this position for over five years now. I bet there are a hundred different little things we could do to knock off 10 seconds here, 15 seconds there — it all adds up into gainshares, you know."

• "Why don't I check back with you a little bit each day and see what we can come up with? It can't hurt anything, can it?"

• "Hey, Rome wasn't built in a day. I'm not saying that you'll jump up 40% tomorrow just by working faster. I'm just saying let's spend a couple months thinking about it, and see what happens."

A lot will happen. The important thing is for the supervisor to mention the 40% goal daily, and to touch base with the employee each day to see if there are any new ideas. A lot of interesting things will happen in the following months.

Step 3: Establishing documentation

Each of the mentored employees needs to have their current productivity levels documented at the beginning of the mentoring.

A clear beginning rate for mentoring is important so that when the mentored employees increase their productivity during the course of the program, it can be tracked as basis points. For example, let's say an employee is currently earning 50 cents on gainshares, their mentor rate at the beginning is 115% of the starting point for Simplified Gainsharing.

Each mentored employee is tracked in this manner, and the basis points of each supervisor's four employees are credited to the supervisor. Whenever the basis points reach 100, the supervisor is eligible for a $2,000 bonus.

PRODUCTIVITY RULE #70

When the team of mentored employees reach 100 basis points, the supervisor is eligible for a bonus.

There are two time parameters that have to be established by each facility. The first is how long to run the first round of mentoring. A good time span for the first round is two months. All basis points a supervisor has achieved are added up, comparing the starting levels to the ending levels. Any supervisor who has achieved 100 or more basis points is eligible for the $2,000 bonus.

The second time parameter is how long the mentored employees have to maintain the increased level of gainshares to keep the supervisor eligible. In other words, you don't want the mentored employees to achieve their increased levels of productivity, and then maintain them only for a week or two. One hopes they will stay at, or close, to these levels. So before the supervisor's bonus is paid, the mentored employees should have demonstrated that they can maintain these levels.

Chapter 16
Mentoring — Past the First Two Months

What happens after you've run mentoring for two months in a facility?

Here's a short list of what you're sure to see in a facility using this program:

• Approximately one third of your supervisors will achieve their 100 basis points and be in line for their $2,000 bonus.

Why not more than one third? Why not 100% of them, for crying out loud? What's wrong with them? All legitimate questions, but quite frankly, there's nothing wrong with the supervisors. It's not an easy task to get employees to increase their productivity 40% in a two-month period. Indeed, it's an audacious task.

If your facility scores with one third of your supervisors in two months, you're doing great. Let's call it round one and go on. All mentored employees have to be managed through the seven stages at their own speed. The important thing is that the mentoring supervisors are consistent in touching base daily with their mentored employees, getting the 40% goal in front of their eyes, and encouraging them to waste less and less time during the production day.

PRODUCTIVITY RULE #71

Expect to eliminate more FTEs than the number of supervisors who make their mentoring goals.

• Approximately 80% of your mentored employees will have raised their gainshare levels above where they were at the beginning of mentoring.

Employees respond well to the daily attention and goal-setting with their supervisors. This is why you'll see a productivity uptick in the majority of the mentored group. Nothing is ever 100%, so odds are you won't hit a home run with each and every employee during the first two months. But 80% will enable you to peel off a substantial number of FTEs.

• The facility manager will have spun off approximately twice as many FTEs as the number of supervisors who qualified for mentoring bonuses.

This statement appears odd at first glance, but perfectly logical when you examine the chart below.

Mentoring Results — Round One			
Facility	Actual Basis Points	FTEs Out the Door Since Mentoring *	Supervisor Bonus Pending
A	402	3	2
B	384	4	0
C	591	5	3
D	296	3	1
E	842	9	4
Total Facilities	2,515	24	10
		$924,000	$20,000
* FTEs removed at $38,500 each			

There are two main reason the numbers are produced in these ratios:

1) Not all supervisors hit 100 basis points in round one, but all supervisors accrue some points. This always results in additional opportunities for the facility to shed FTEs. For example, if the facility has ten supervisors who all achieve fifty basis points in round one, then the facility will have attained 500 basis points, or the opportunity to shed five FTEs, without any supervisor achieving a $2,000 bonus.

PRODUCTIVITY RULE #72

Mentoring creates ancillary labor hours saved beyond the original mentored group of employees.

2) Ideas that help the mentored group also assist all the other non-mentored employees. For example, if a mentored employee creates a tunnel in an aisle or moves 10 SKUs into a golden zone for picking, these improvements would also help the other employees in the department. As a consequence, there are ancillary productivity improvements beyond the mentoring groups that create additional saved labor hours. These create more opportunities to shed FTEs.

Clearly the cost justification of mentoring is weighted heavily in favor of the company. Checking out the chart above, we find that the company is in the enviable position of shedding $924,000 of labor costs while incurring a supervisory bonus payout level of $20,000. Anyone would agree this is a pretty darn good ROI.

So we suggest continuing the supervisors' opportunity to earn the original $2,000 bonus by extending the basis point accumulation into round two. The rules are simple. Just allow the supervisors to each pick a second team to mentor and run round two the same way you ran round one.

The only difference is that the supervisors accumulate basis points from both the original team and the new team. For example, here are a supervisor's results from round one:

Mentoring Results — Round One				
Group A				
Employee One	Employee Two	Employee Three	Employee Four	TOTAL
20	15	40	10	85

This supervisor just missed the 100 basis points and the $2,000 bonus during round one. Going into round two, the supervisor picks a second team of employees to mentor, while retaining the first team, which now requires considerably less time. After round two is completed, we see that the original team continued to increase their productivity in months three and four, and are now significantly above their starting point.

As a consequence, the original team provided 130 points — more than enough for a $2,000 bonus. When added to the supervisor's second team, the supervisor now has enough basis points to earn two bonuses, for a total of $4,000.

Mentoring Results — Round One Employees				
Group A				
Employee One	Employee Two	Employee Three	Employee Four	TOTAL
35	20	50	25	130

Mentoring Results — Round Two Employees				
Group A				
Employee One	Employee Two	Employee Three	Employee Four	TOTAL
10	15	30	25	80

Grand Total	210

Mentoring — Rounds Three & Four

Where do you stop?

Stop only when all supervisors fail to continue earning $2,000 bonuses, and it's clear there are no more productivity advances to be wrung out of your facility. But be prepared to be surprised with just how far these mentoring exercises can go, and just how many FTEs can be jettisoned due to the increased productivity accomplishments of the individuals in your facility.

You can easily roll into round three, round four, and even further. Run these rounds in the same way you've run the first two rounds, and allow the supervisors to accumulate basis points from all the rounds combined. Remember it's to your advantage to pay out $2,000 bonuses, because each time you do, you remove an FTE from your workforce. But the mentoring program is not akin to Simplified Gainsharing in that it can't be perpetuated forever in your DC. While individual workers can continue to earn gainshares indefinitely, with mentoring you're eventually going to hit a point where FTEs cannot be removed.

PRODUCTIVITY RULE #73

Mentoring is so lucrative for the company that supervisors should be provided additional opportunities to earn the $2,000 bonus.

When that point is reached, your facility should be close to the ultimate audacious goal, and your productivity should be at levels that are doubled over where your facility started Simplified Gainsharing. Going back to our model facility, your FTE graph should be in similar proportions to the one below:

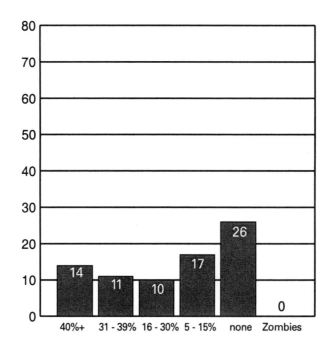

In this particular example, the facility started with 141 employees, and is down to 78 at this point in its productivity growth. The facility's sales increased in the four-year time span, which coupled with the FTE reduction resulted in a 100%+ increase in productivity.

And what can be done with a single facility, can be done with an entire network. It might take more than four years for the whole network, but the point needs to be made that every corporate sponsor should embrace the ultimate audacious goal and shoot for the doubling of network productivity. Of course it sounds audacious . . . but it can be done!

Chapter 17
Mentoring — Questions & Answers

Question: Many supervisors appear to struggle to attain enough basis points to receive the bonus. However, they still manage to carve out an FTE or two from their departments. Is it okay to credit them with more basis points than those accrued only by their mentored employees?

Answer: Of course. The main goal of mentoring is to create ways to jettison FTEs while retaining the ability to efficiently process the facility volume. There are several ways a supervisor can remove FTEs from the department, and he or she should be rewarded for removing FTEs even if the method doesn't fall into the pre-established expectations.

Question: What are some of these ways?

Answer: Clearly, the productivity increases by individual workers are the key to painless FTE removal (remember the example of 100 employees who each increase their productivity 10%, enabling the facility to process the same volume with 90 employees). There are two main ways mentoring aids the goal of individual productivity increases beyond the mentored group:

1) Ancillary increases in the mentored employees' work group. Process ideas developed by mentored employees help all the employees in the work group or department. For example, a tunnel to aid work flow helps everyone, not just the mentored employee who thought of the tunnel. Another ancillary impact is seen where some non-mentored employees mimic the productivity increases of the mentored group, who raise the departmental awareness that higher gainshares are indeed attainable.

2) As the above developments occur, they ultimately increase the potential for buying out the entire department.

Question: So you would pay the supervisor a $2,000 bonus even though the 100 basis points were not attained?

Answer: Yes. The goal is FTE removal, not necessarily the attainment of 100 basis points. Supervisors have to work hard with their entire department to eliminate an FTE, whether by implementing process ideas or conducting buyout discussions. If they can pop out an FTE, they deserve the $2,000. Besides, calculate what an FTE costs you annually in wages and benefits, and we think you'll agree that $2,000 is a small price to pay to save this dollar amount.

Question: What if the facility is in a period of declining sales or volume? Aren't you going to remove FTEs as a natural consequence of declining volume?

Answer: Yes, and $2,000 bonuses should not be paid for downsizing or layoffs. Remember the idea here is to pay for only productivity increases that enable the supervisor to process the same workloads with less people in the same time periods. So bonus determinations should only be made on the criteria of departmental productivity gains.

Question: Isn't mentoring a form of bounty hunting? Do we really want to create an atmosphere of paying bonuses to eliminate people?

Answer: We imagine it could be seen in this negative light. So you must manage past such adverse concepts. Most facilities have enough turnover or volume gains to achieve FTE removal painlessly. The atmosphere you want to create in your facility is one where every salaried employee is completely wired into continuing productivity increases coupled with prolonged FTE removal. This is the ideal culture or atmosphere for the best financial gains for the company, and there's nothing as important as a strong company for the continued well-being of the workforce.

Question: But these principles do not necessarily promote the well-being of all employees. You say no one should be hurt by Simplified Gainsharing or mentoring, yet layoffs do indeed adversely impact some employees.

Answer: True. Layoffs should only be used as a last resort, to be used when no FTEs are being removed by attrition or the increased use of free time. In non-union facilities, layoffs should be conducted based on performance criteria. In this case, the employees laid off are those who are performing at levels inferior to the rest of the workforce. In union facilities, layoffs are unfortunately conducted by seniority. As such, recently hired employees who might be performing at higher levels than others in the workforce are the ones laid off. Sometimes this situation can be avoided by asking more senior people to volunteer for the layoff — on rare occasions more senior people may agree to take a layoff in order to go on unemployment.

Layoffs in this context should be distinguished from terminations which are the result of defined and ongoing disciplinary procedures which may be related to safety, absenteeism, performance, quality or other factors specific to the individual organization and independent of productivity improvement processes.

Question: How far do you go with mentoring and buyouts? When does it end? What's the top in performance?

Answer: The top of performance is different for all companies. None of us really know the top end of human performance. But we think one of the signs of the top is when a work group cannot completely recover the previous gainshare levels from the last buyout. This point is probably a pretty good sign the work group is maxed in its present context.

Question: Do you then buyout the last gainshare levels?

Answer: No. At this point you have a superior work group. You eliminated a ton of FTEs. In this light, the employees who have brought you to this point deserve to be paid at exemplary rates. Also, your turnover rates at this point should be well below 5%; paying employees exemplary rates will keep them in your organization. Actually, you've achieved a major goal with the work group — the employees are working at their top performance, and the company is attaining full value for the wages it's paying.

Question: Any final ideas to help boost mentoring?

Answer: Here are two. Use the mentored employees as trainers of other employees who are trying to raise their gainshares. It's a great way to cement both the current gains and the determination of the mentored employees. The second idea is to video a mentored employee for a half hour or so, then play the film back to the same employee (a small caution here is to keep the video confidential in order not to expose the employee to possible jokes from coworkers; it should only be shown to the mentored employee who was the subject of the video). It's amazing how even the best employees will find things to change or techniques to improve when viewing their work like this. Supervisors and employees who have tried this video idea have reported back that it's definitely worth the time out of the work day to analyze these films.

Chapter 18
Afterword

So that's our story — told as straight-forwardly as we could manage — about methods to greatly increase performance to the point of doubling the productivity of facilities and networks. In the end, it's all about how to resurrect your workforce. Now let's see if we can distill the essence of the whole book into a few simple paragraphs.

The overarching premise of the book is: You currently have potential banshees and super-banshees among both your hourly workforce and your salaried ranks. These people are already in place, and the Simplified Gainsharing principles can bring these individuals to their full potential. In other words, you can move significant groups of your blue-collar employees from standard productivity to hyper-productivity. Likewise, you can move most of your salaried employees, the executives and managers responsible for profit attainment, from satisfaction with the current norm to embracing the ultimate audacious goal of doubling productivity. You don't have to search the world to hire great employees — you already have all the banshees you'll ever need.

When you start to apply Simplified Gainsharing principles, you'll quickly see how the Seven Stages of Managerial Death are evident throughout the entire company, with various levels of employees exhibiting different stages and degrees of evolution at various times. And all employees will require assistance in managing themselves through the seven stages to attain acceptance.

In the end, your endeavor is to create a culture change in both the individual facilities and the executive and corporate teams. Productivity levels accepted as the norm at the beginning of the process will later come to be viewed as anemic. Goal setting for profit attainment will be forever changed. As the workforce grows stronger and stronger over the years, so too will the company's financial strength become herculean.

It all starts with the decision to create sliding scales with no caps.

Be brave. Be audacious. Waste no time!

Sample Plan Document

Many distribution professionals that we have spoken with have been interested in obtaining electronic versions of the plan document and charts included in these appendices.

The authors are happy to send out electronic versions to any of their readers. Feel free to contact Pat Kelley at ward708@aol.com or Ron Hounsell at r.hounsell@comcast.net. We also invite you to visit the Simplified Gainsharing websites: www.gainshares.com and www.labordevelopmentgroup.com.

Distribution Center Simplified Gainsharing Plan

Objectives:

Simplified Gainsharing is a blue-collar incentive program designed to motivate individual employees to increase their productivity and quality. The deliverable of the Simplified Gainsharing Program is increased performance of the facility as measured by overall facility productivity, turnover, and quality measurements.

Eligibility:

All employees who can be measured individually for productivity and quality are eligible to earn monthly gainshares as described in the plan. Included are the following departments: Receiving, Putaway, Hand Stock & Life Stock, Replenishment, Orderfilling, Shipping, Quality Control, and Cycle Counts.

Certain employees can only be measured as a team, and their ability to earn monthly gainshares will be based on team measurements or overall facility productivity and quality. Included are the following departments: Maintenance, Office, Slotting/Binsizing, New Goods, and Janitorial.

Payouts:

All payouts will be paid on a monthly basis, based on departmental sliding scales with no caps. To earn a gainshare, the individual must attain one of the levels on the sliding scales as outlined in this document. This is done by achieving a monthly productivity and/or quality level. Once the level has been achieved for a month, a gainshare raise will be applied to the employee's hourly rate for all hours worked in the following month, including vacation, sick pay, holiday, and overtime hours. Productivity and quality will be reviewed on a monthly basis; if the employee maintains the gainshare level, the raise will continue. If the employee achieves a higher gainshare level for a month, the appropriate raise will be applied; if the employee performs at a rate below the sliding scale payouts, the employee's wage rate will revert to the appropriate lower rate or the original standard rate of pay before any gainshare was achieved.

Components:

The Simplified Gainsharing program can be modified or terminated by the Company at any time in the event it is found to be unsuccessful in its goal of improving facility efficiencies. In the event such modification is necessary, management will make a good-faith effort to work in conjunction with the employees and departments involved.

All departments of the Distribution Center have Productivity sliding scales and Quality qualifiers, and are outlined in this Plan document.

The Plan contains a Buyout procedure, which is used in the event of capital or process improvements that require a re-adjustment of the sliding scales in a manner that is fair to both the employees and the Company. The Buyout procedure is outlined at the end of the Plan document.

An employee's Home Base will be determined by that section or area where the employee spends the majority of the work week. Since gainshares are calculated by a percentage above a baseline in a particular section, a home base is needed to determine an employee's gainshare level.

Following are the gainshare plans for the DC's departments. For all job classifications, there are certain requirements and restrictions:

• To be eligible, 51% of hours worked must be in Home Base.

• Failure to hit quality qualifier will eliminate any incentive payouts.

• Any falsifications of production or quality will not only eliminate any incentive gainshares but will also be grounds for termination.

• There is no "double dipping" — payouts will be made only for the area in which you spent 51% or more of your work hours.

*** *To be eligible, lead people must work 65% of their hours in a productivity function.* ***

*** *This program may be modified or terminated at any time.* ***

Receiving

The receiver's job is to receive all incoming goods. In doing so, he or she must:

• Work marked-out lines and/or oldest freight first

• Follow proper procedures for detailed check-in, packing list check-in, or certified vendor

• Prepare freight in a quality manner to be sent to appropriate forwards or reserves

• Stage freight in hold areas.

The following list of point assignments should be applied each day to determine your production rate.

• One point for each line completed receiving work sheet

• Two points for each line completed as a detailed check-in

• One point for each pallet placed in hold area.

LINES PER HOUR (LPH) ABOVE BASE		10%	15%	20%	25%	30%	35%	40%	45%	50%
Gainshare payouts		$.25	$.50	$.75	$1.00	$1.25	$1.50	$1.75	$2.00	$2.25
ACTIVITY	Base									
DPA	15	6.5	17	18	19	19.5	20	21	22	22.5
UPS	16	17.5	18	19	20	21	21.5	22	23	24
TSP	11	12	12.5	13	13.5	14	15	15.5	16	16.5

There are no caps on the levels of gainshares, and the above example continues in 5% increments; for example, 55% will earn $2.50, and so on.

The quality qualifier is no more than the following:

Maximum Gainshare Possible	10%	15%	20%	25%	30%	35%	40%	45%	50%
Maximum Errors	6	7	8	9	10	11	12	12	12

These include errors found by inventory control or quality associates during auditing, including but not limited to:

• Any mis-stocked bins

• Reserves in the wrong location

• Any incorrect quantities

• Failure to cut shrink wrap or strapping from pallets

• Opening full case picks

• Not removing and opening inner cartons

• Inventory incident reports

• Any type of error on a receiving worksheet or reserve ticket

• Not getting approval for packing list check-in

• Not filling out an OS&D when necessary

• Cutting corners at another's expense.

Hand Stock — Job and Point Structure

The stocker's job is to stock all incoming goods. In doing so, he or she must:

• Work oldest freight first

• Make sure the forward bins are full before creating reserves

• Date your primary reserve with the oldest date

• Primary reserves should contain enough to fill the forward.

The following list of procedures should be applied each day to determine your production rate:

• One point for each line filled on the replenishment sheet

• One point for each Delete when stocking or handling a Picker's Drop

• One point for each Add

• One point for each line filled on a receiving worksheet and put into the forward bin.

LINES PER HOUR (LPH) ABOVE BASE		10%	15%	20%	25%	30%	35%	40%	45%	50%
Gainshare payouts		$.25	$.50	$.75	$1.00	$1.25	$1.50	$1.75	$2.00	$2.25
SECTION	Base									
Repo	15	16.5	17	18	19	19.5	20	21	22	22.5
Hand	16	17.5	18	19	20	21	21.5	22	23	24
Drops	11	12	12.5	13	13.5	14	15	15.5	16	16.5

There are no caps on the levels of gainshares, and the above example continues in 5% increments; for example, 55% will earn $2.50, and so on.

The quality qualifier is no more than the following:

Maximum Gainshare Possible	10%	15%	20%	25%	30%	35%	40%	45%	50%
Maximum Errors	6	7	8	9	10	11	12	12	12

The following constitutes an error in hand stocking:

• Forward bin not filled to capacity

• Not cutting open cartons

• Any mis-stocked bins

• Any reserve add error

• Any incorrect quantities

• Reserves in the wrong locations

• Handwriting or clock number illegible

• Failure to note discrepancies on receiving worksheet

• Any errors found by supervisors or assistant supervisors.

Lift Stock — Job and Point Structure

The stocker's job is to stock all incoming goods. In doing so, he or she must:

• Work oldest freight first

• Make sure the forward bins are full before creating reserves

• Empty bins should be swept out and cleared of all debris before new pallet is put in.

The following should be applied each day to determine your production rate:

• One point for each line filled on the replenishment sheet.

• One point for each Delete when stocking or handling a Picker's Drop.

• One point for each Add

• One point for each line filled on a Receiving Worksheet and put into the forward bin.

LINES PER HOUR (LPH) ABOVE BASE		10%	15%	20%	25%	30%	35%	40%	45%	50%
Gainshare payouts		$.25	$.50	$.75	$1.00	$1.25	$1.50	$1.75	$2.00	$2.25
SECTION	**Base**									
Repo	15	16.5	17	18	19	19.5	20	21	22	22.5
Hand	16	17.5	18	19	20	21	21.5	22	23	24
Drops	11	12	12.5	13	13.5	14	15	15.5	16	16.5

There are no caps on the levels of gainshares, and the above example continues in 5% increments; for example, 55% will earn $2.50, and so on.

The quality qualifier is no more than the following:

Maximum Gainshare Possible	10%	15%	20%	25%	30%	35%	40%	45%	50%
Maximum Errors	6	7	8	9	10	11	12	12	12

The following constitutes an error in replenishment stocking:

• Forward bin not filled to capacity

• Not cutting shrink wrap or strapping

• Any mis-stocked bins

• Any reserve add error

• Any incorrect quantities

• Reserves in the wrong locations

• Handwriting and clock number illegible

• Failure to note discrepancies on receiving worksheet

• Any errors found by supervisors or assistant supervisors.

Orderfilling

% ABOVE BASE		5%	10%	15%	20%	25%	30%	35%	40%	45%
Gainshare payouts		$.25	$.50	$.75	$1.00	$1.25	$1.50	$1.75	$2.00	$2.25
ZONE	Base									
1	130	143	150	156	163	169	176	182	189	195
2	120	132	138	144	150	156	162	168	174	180
3	115	127	133	138	144	150	156	161	167	173
4	130	143	150	156	163	169	176	182	189	195
5	70	77	81	84	88	91	95	98	102	105
6	250	275	288	300	313	325	338	350	363	375
7	65	72	75	78	82	85	88	91	95	98
8	45	50	52	54	57	59	61	63	66	68
9	15	17	19	21	23	25	27	29	31	33
10	60	66	69	72	75	78	81	84	87	90
11	60	66	69	72	75	78	81	84	87	90
12	35	39	41	43	45	47	49	51	53	55
13	85	94	98	102	107	111	115	119	124	128
14	130	143	150	156	163	169	176	182	189	195

There are no caps on the levels of gainshares, and the above example continues in 5% increments; for example, 50% will earn $2.50, and so on.

The above zone quality qualifier is . 40 full case and .60 repack.

Super Quality				
Eligible in Orderfilling sections ONLY				
		1st Month	2nd Month	3rd Month
0.25%	Repack	$0.50	$0.50	$0.50
0.15%	Full Case	$0.50	$0.50	$0.50

There will be a cumulative cap at $1.50 extra per hour for super quality.

• Failure to make the production base will eliminate any incentive payouts.

• For repack areas if an orderfiller who has achieved a level of super quality falls between a .25 and a .60 for the month they will lose one level ($0.50 per hour)for the next month. If an orderfiller who has achieved a level of super quality has a monthly quality average of greater than .60 they will lose all levels they have earned (up to $1.50 per hour) for the next month.

• If a full case area orderfiller who has achieved a level of super quality falls between a .15 and a .40 for the month they will lose one level ($0.50 per hour) for the next month. If an orderfiller who has achieved a level of super quality has a monthly quality average of greater than a .40 they will lose all levels they have earned (up to $1.50 per hour) for the next month.

Quality Control

LPH ABOVE BASE		10%	15%	20%	25%	30%	35%	40%	45%	50%
Incentive payouts		$.25	$.50	$.75	$1.00	$1.25	$1.50	$1.75	$2.00	$2.25
SECTION	Base									
QC Loop	150	165	172	180	187.5	195	202.5	210	217.5	225
QC Cart	75	82.5	86	90	94	97.5	101	105	109	112.5

There will be no cap to the productivity incentive, which will continue in 5% increments.

The quality qualifier is no more than the following:

Maximum Gainshare Possible	10%	15%	20%	25%	30%	35%	40%	45%	50%
Maximum Errors	6	7	8	9	10	11	12	12	12

The following constitutes an error in Quality Control:

• Any errors found by inventory control during auditing, including but not limited to:

 – Any incorrect quantities

 – Inventory incident reports

 – Totes or shorts not being filled correctly.

• Any errors found by supervisors, assistant supervisors, lead people, shipping, or claims processing.

Shipping

% ABOVE BASE	10%	15%	20%	25%	30%	35%	40%	45%
Incentive payouts	$.25	$.50	$.75	$1.00	$1.25	$1.50	$1.75	$2.00
Base: 3750 WPH	4125	4313	4500	4688	4875	5063	5250	5438

Authorized returns/UPS

% ABOVE BASE	10%	15%	20%	25%	30%	35%	40%	45%
Base: 20 LINES/ PH	22	23	24	25	26	27	28	29

There will be no cap to the productivity incentive, which will continue in 5% increments.

The loaders' quality qualifier is: maintain a monthly average score of 75 or above.

Load quality is based on the drivers' reports provided by the transportation department.

Office, Maintenance, Slotting/Binsizing, New Goods, Cycle Counts, and Porter/Janitor

Certain classifications are unique, in that there are no specific productivity measurements for these positions. However, these positions are important and do influence the overall productivity of the facility. When the associates in these classifications perform their functions effectively, the entire facility benefits. Team gainshares can be calculated by a DC-wide measurement such as throughput.

Throughput dollars is a key measurement used to gauge the productivity of the distribution center. Throughput dollars are calculated using the following formula:

$$\frac{\text{(Sales dollars)} + \text{(Inbound dollars)} + \text{(Transfer and Debit dollars)}}{\text{Hours Worked in Facility Excluding Vacation and Holiday Hours}} = \text{Throughput dollars per Hour}$$

% ABOVE BASE	5%	10%	15%	20%	25%	30%	35%
Gainshare	$.25	$.50	$.75	$1.00	$1.25	$1.50	$1.75
Base 800	840	880	920	960	1000	1040	1080

There will be no cap to the productivity incentive, which will continue in 5% increments.

Buyouts

Periodically the overall productivity of the distribution center sections and departments will need to be reviewed by supervisors and the employees.

As we continue to improve our efficiencies year by year, capital or process improvements might require a readjustment of the sliding scales in a manner that is fair to both the employees and the company. The actual dollar amounts of the lump-sum bonus of the buyout and the actual amount of the sliding scale bought out will be determined by a consensus of departmental supervision and the employees currently earning gainshares.

An example of a buyout would be if the department is provided new equipment (e.g., new tow motors) that automatically increase the overall productivity by 10%. After discussions between the supervisor and the tow motor drivers earning gainshares, it is determined that an equitable buyout is a $200 lump-sum check for each employee in the tow motor department (regardless of whether they are currently earning gainshares or not), which buys the company the ability to move the starting point of the sliding scales upward 10%. This effectively buys out the first two levels of gainshares and allows the gainsharing program to readjust its sliding scales fairly to a level commensurate with the original starting points.

The company will not unilaterally buy out levels; this is always done by consensus of supervision and gainshare employees. Also, no starting point will be adjusted upward where it automatically places an employee below the disciplinary point for that department. The objective with buyouts is to periodically fairly adjust the gainsharing program so that it can continue to provide its intended efficiencies.

Metrics and Baselines

Some managers feel it's unwise to rely solely on hourly employees, or any other single source, as the basis for establishing metrics. People can only tell you what they know from their experience, and many hourly warehouse employees know only one or two scenarios on which to draw to answer this kind of question. Expertise in this context can be a very important factor in determining the success or failure for the entire project.

If you're setting baselines in departments within a network, it's easy to get a reality check on your employees' recommendations simply by comparing similar departments in other facilities. If you're dealing with a Greenfield (a newly built facility), it's wise to seek the guidance of industrial engineers.

Another effective method is called the "Step Up" method. It lends itself well to Greenfield departments where you have a good idea of the desired baseline by comparing the new department to like-departments in other facilities; it also lends itself well to capital improvement installations where an increase in productivity has been targeted.

The best way to describe the Step Up method is to simply illustrate two examples of its successful application (the following are not the real company names).

Example One

The Apex Company built a 900,000-sq.-ft. greenfield that contained 10 flow rack sections. From its network experience, Apex knew the productivity in its flow racks averaged 100 lines per hour (lph). However, the managers who laid out the Greenfield used new slotting software that precisely laid out the 10 flow racks in a pristine "golden zone" manner. As a result, they projected the Greenfield flow racks should easily average 110 lph, or 10% higher than the network average.

Past experience also indicated that it took approximately three months for an orderfiller hired "off the street" to come up to full productivity. Using the Step Up method, Apex managers implemented the

Time from start	Baseline	Start for 1st 25 cent gainshare
1st month	60	63
2nd month	75	79
3rd month	100	105
4th month	110	116

sliding scale at right for Simplified Gainsharing at the greenfield.

As you can see, Apex stepped up the baseline over a four-month period, giving the new orderfillers three months to build up to the projection of 110 lph. Apex started each month's gainshares at 5% above the baseline. The new employees responded so well to this method that the flow racks in the Greenfield were averaging 121 lph after the four-month process. The baseline then stayed at 110 until a regular buyout was performed later in the year.

Example Two

The Generic Warehouse leased $1 million worth of new forklifts for its East Coast facility. These new lifts traveled 8% faster than the average old lifts at Generic, and the mastheads moved up and down at a much quicker rate.

Generic managers decided to use the Step Up method to attain a 10% increase in forklift productivity. They developed an aggressive communication and training program so the employees would understand the cost to the company of the new equipment and the performance upticks the new lifts would provide. The current baseline for forklift productivity was 20 lph, but this was now outdated due to the new lifts. However, to be fair to the lift drivers, the company implemented the sliding scales at right.

Time from start	Baseline	Start for 1st 25 cent gainshare
1st month	20	22
2nd month	20.5	22.5
3rd month	21	23
4th month	22	24.2

From the above chart, you can see Generic stepped up the baseline over a four-month period, giving the lift drivers three months to build up to their projection of 22 lph. Generic started each month's gainshares at approximately 10% above the baseline. The lift drivers thought the Step Up process was more than fair, and responded favorably to the capital improvement. Later into the year, the whole group of lift drivers was bought out at the 25% level.

Supervisor's Checklist

Below is a checklist for supervisors who are administering a Simplified Gainsharing program in their departments. When considering all the layers of a corporation, the most critical interaction concerning Simplified Gainsharing takes place between the line supervisors and the blue-collar workers. We suggest it's a good idea to print this list out, and have the supervisory staff consider its points together on a weekly basis. It might also be a good topic for regular supervisory meetings.

- Daily Contact

- Use Their Ideas

- Circled Dollar Amounts

- Interdepartmental Touching

- Personal Enthusiasm Reality Check

- Corporate sponsor $20 Recommendation

- Departmental Comparison

Let's flesh each of these out. Basically, the items on the supervisor's checklist are the critical daily tools that need to be in every supervisor's toolbox. There are many different techniques for motivating employees, and the list is not meant to be all-inclusive. The most important thing is that supervisors intensively interact with their employees during the Simplified Gainsharing installation.

Daily Contact ("Touching")

The essence of supervision lies in one's ability to motivate a work group toward achieving the best results — the best productivity, quality, and safety — possible. In a sense, it's similar to being the coach of a sports team, although a supervisor faces a more difficult task to rally the team around a common flag.

But like the coach, the supervisor must "touch base" with each of the employees on the work team on a daily basis. A supervisor can't motivate people by remote control; instead, the supervisor needs to be constantly out on the lines, working the crowds like a politician seeking votes.

While everyone on a sports team has the common goal of winning the game, the employees in a work group all have different reasons for becoming banshees. It's true they are all at the company to earn a living, but anyone can show up for work. The task before the supervisor is to discover which button to push for each employee, discover the reason that will motivate them to try for higher and higher gainshare levels. This is right at the core of great supervision; scratch any successful supervisor and you'll find someone skilled at understanding blue-collar behavior and motivation.

And here's the rub in many companies — while it's essential that supervisors speak with their employees on a daily basis, many supervisors have been loaded up with paperwork or out-and-out bureaucracy, and simply don't have the time to touch base with their employees each day. However, inspired companies make certain their supervisors have blocks of time during the day dedicated to touching base with their employees, particularly if a Simplified Gainsharing program is being installed.

How much time? And what should they be talking about?

It's simple — we're only talking about a few minutes each day with each employee. The "touch" could focus on the employee's productivity from yesterday, or quality numbers, or even the ballgame last night; but somewhere in there a personal goal or departmental goal should be slipped in, and the supervisor should jet off to the next employee. It doesn't take long, but it lets all the employees know they're important, and the departmental goals are important. Besides, it quickly gives the supervisor a current read on how the entire department is doing.

Employees who are not touched daily eventually slide into some form of mediocrity. Even employees who stay above the minimum — for even 15% above expectation is mediocre for a super-banshee, isn't it?

Use Their Ideas

Here's our favorite story on this topic, a real-life incident from the front lines of supervision: A young supervisor fielded an idea from his department one day, concerning installing a static conveyor line from one power conveyor to another. The idea was that it would allow employees to roll a tote from one picking line to another instead of carrying the totes, as they currently were.

Not a terrible idea, but the supervisor didn't think it would make much of an impact on departmental productivity. So it's not surprising to note that when the supervisor did the ROI calculation on the conveyor installation, there was not much of a payback. After doing the calculation, the supervisor told the department that it just didn't make sense to install the conveyor.

The workers looked astounded, and certainly didn't believe the conveyor would be nearly useless. They assured the supervisor the conveyor would be a significant aid to the department.

The supervisor said it just didn't make sense.

One employee retorted that the conveyor would help them increase their productivity at least 10%. It didn't make a dent on the supervisor, and soon the meeting was brought to a close.

Later that week, the supervisor mentioned the incident to the facility manager, and derided the 10% number. The supervisor went over the ROI calculations, and all the reasons the conveyor would be ineffective. The manager listened closely to the facts the supervisor related, then smiled and said, "It might sound shocking what I'm going to advise, but I think you should go ahead with the conveyor installation." When the supervisor looked stunned, the manager explained, "More times than not, when you use the employees' ideas, they will make it work. I know it's not mathematically sound, but it works. Call it a self-fulfilled prophecy, or call it pride of authorship — most times employees will make their ideas work come hell or high water."

In the end, the young supervisor installed the static conveyor, and was astounded to see the departmental productivity increase over 10% within a couple of weeks. The facility manager had been absolutely correct. The 10% increase was sustained for many months, until the supervisor fielded another idea for improvement from the people and was able to drive their production even higher.

So the moral of the story is clear: Whenever possible, use the employees' ideas, even though the math might be against the idea. As long as the idea doesn't cost a fortune or go against company policy, it's wise to go along with what the employees suggest. It's just human nature to make the ideas you espouse work so that you're proven right.

Circled Dollar Amounts

This is a simple idea, but very effective. When a supervisor begins implementing a Simplified Gainsharing program in a department, constant feedback is the most effective way to increase the employees' individual productivity. This is why we so strongly recommend touching base daily. Another great way to give feedback to individual employees is by calculating their productivity levels from the prior day, then applying it to the appropriate gainshare level. For instance, if the employee was working at a 20% increase rate the prior day, the employee would earn a full $1 raise if this level were maintained for a month.

The idea is to write down the $1 amount on today's productivity tabulation, the employee's production record, or some other format where the employee can be individually noted. Many supervisors circle the gainshare amounts so their employees can readily understand the raises they might be earning in the following month. It's a good way to give employees feedback on the potential gainshare rates they could earn.

Interdepartmental Touching

Daily touching is great, circling the potential gainshare amount is great, but there's another way to make a tremendous impact on an employee who is in the process of becoming a banshee or super-banshee. When an employee hits a superlative level of productivity, not only should that employee's supervisor do the "touch," but some other supervisors in the facility should seek out the employee and praise the achievement.

There's nothing quite as impactful on an employee's morale than another supervisor or manager taking the time to go up to the employee and say they heard about the achievement in a supervisors' meeting. It will leave a lasting impression on the employee.

Personal Enthusiasm Reality Check

This is a relatively basic idea in the world of supervision, but it's worth repeating. An important part of the art of supervision is the ability to motivate employees by an infectious attitude toward the goal the supervisor is trying to accomplish. So it doesn't hurt for supervisors to periodically question themselves concerning whether or not they're at the top of their game concerning enthusiasm.

Supervisors need to enthusiastically reinforce certain principles with individual employees on a daily basis. Such principles include:

• Individual incentives are much better than team incentives.

• Every employee should have a specific gainshare goal.

• Circle a dollar amount on employees' productivity sheets.

• Ask employees for ideas to improve their gainshares.

• Free time might be a better motivator than money.

• Find new ways each week to disseminate the gainshare message.

• Be creative.

The point we're trying to make here is the degree of success a facility will have with Simplified Gainsharing is critically contingent on the skills and interaction of the supervisory staff with the blue-collar employees. Enthusiasm is the oil that makes this machinery whirl!

Corporate Sponsor $20 Recommendation

This is one of our favorite motivational techniques, mostly because it provides such a memorable event for the employees involved.

When the corporate sponsor or a vice president visits the facility, each supervisor hands in the name of one of their employees who has done something outstanding recently. Preferably the recommendation would be for a gainshare level attained, or an exemplary quality rate, or even a demonstration of superb teamwork.

The corporate sponsor then goes down to the floor with the facility manager and is introduced to each employee by their department supervisor, one at a time. It might go something like this:

Supervisor: "Fred, I'd like to introduce you to John Smith, our VP of Logistics. John, this is Fred Jones, one of the most productive coworkers in my department. Last month, Fred was 140% above standard, and is now earning a $2.00 an hour raise on his gainshares."

Corporate Sponsor: "Fred, I'm very happy to meet you. When I was at the supervisors' meeting this morning, I asked the supervisors if they had any great employees downstairs, and if they did, I wanted to go down and meet them. Your supervisor was very excited about me coming down to meet you, Fred. I just wanted to shake your hand, and tell you that I'm very glad you're working for our company. Employees like you are the backbone of our corporation.

"Also, I'd like you to do me a favor today, Fred, and go out and have lunch on the company with this $20 bill. And thanks again for choosing to work in our facility."

This is guaranteed to make a great impression on any of your employees, and it's something they'll remember the rest of their careers. Not to mention, you'll get your $20 back in the next day or two in the increased productivity this form of recognition produces.

Departmental Comparison

The best supervisors are continually comparing their departments with the same department in other facilities in the network. They want their department to be number one. In their minds, there's only one place to be — number one.

Number one is a place that cannot be reached by the back door. You can't sidle up to number one, nor can you arrive there by accident. The best supervisors know this, and are not shy about stating their ambition for their departments. They tell their employees they want the department to be number one. They have the courage to put themselves on the line, and simply put, this verbal statement of the goal is how everyone who has achieved number one has started. You must have the gumption to enunciate it.

The next step after enunciation is comparison. You must tell your employees where they stand compared to the best department. Most networks keep departmental comparisons among facilities, but if the network doesn't keep a monthly comparison, the supervisor can certainly start one by calling his counterparts in other facilities.

It's not surprising that all the best supervisors are focused on this comparison; perhaps what is surprising is how their workforces have rallied to this same intense focus on attaining the status of being the best in the network.

Gainshare Impact Charts

For a successful Simplified Gainsharing program, it is essential that you get employee buy-in. One way to do that is to show employees how Simplified Gainsharing will benefit them. You can use the charts on the next two pages (or develop similar charts to match the specifics of your program) to illustrate to employees the benefits of Simplified Gainsharing.

This chart shows the impact of gainshares on a 40-hour paycheck.

For those individuals who would rather go fishing, this chart shows how much time off per week an employee could take and still earn a "40-hour" check.

Mentoring Plan Document

Following is a sample mentoring plan document. You can use this document as is, or modify it to meet your needs.

Objectives:

Mentoring is an ancillary supervisory bonus program designed to incentivize supervisors to increase the productivity of selected employees. The deliverable of the Mentoring Program is the removal of FTEs from the Distribution Center's workforce by increasing overall productivity.

Payouts:

As judged by the Operating Manager, each supervisor will be paid a one-time $2,000 bonus for each FTE they remove from the workforce.

Mentoring Components:

1) Supervisor's Team

• Each supervisor will select a team of four or five employees to mentor toward increased levels of productivity. The Mentoring effort should be done in one-on-one conversations for approximately 15 minutes each day on how to improve productivity. Ideally these short meetings would occur on the floor.

• If longer meetings are required to discuss ideas in depth, it might be appropriate to take the employee off the floor.

• As the Mentoring round progresses through the weeks, the daily contact meetings might only require a minute or two.

2) Team Selection

• First the supervisory staff should determine whether they will select interdepartmentally, or only from their own department.

• If the selection is limited to only those employees within a supervisor's department, each supervisor can proceed to select his or her own Mentoring Team.

• If the interdepartmental method is selected, the first selection from each supervisor should be limited to their own department, so that they have the opportunity to select the best employee from their department. After this round has been completed, the selection process can proceed "round-robin," with each supervisor picking one employee from the Distribution Center's workforce (regardless of department) until all supervisors have selected their Mentoring team.

• After the initial selection process is completed, trades are allowed if the supervisors want to augment their teams by negotiating with their fellow supervisors.

• Once the supervisors have pre-selected their teams, they must talk to each of the employees they selected, to make certain they want to participate in the Mentoring Program.

• If some employees decide they do not want to participate in the Mentoring Program, those supervisors impacted can then select additional employees to fill out their Mentoring Teams.

3. Basis Point Measurements

• Once the teams have been selected, and Mentoring is ready to begin, the productivity level of each team participant needs to be memorialized. The recommended productivity level used is the employee's production level from the prior four weeks, provided this represents a normal work load. In this manner, benchmarks (or starting points) are established for each Mentored employee.

• These levels are then used to determine how many basis points the supervisor has created with the team during the Mentoring round. *Example:* An employee at the start of Mentoring is at 115% of standard, and at the end of the Mentoring period, the employee is at 140% of standard. The supervisor would receive 25 basis points for this mentored employee (140-115 = 25).

• When the Mentoring round ends, all the mentored employees on the supervisor's team are analyzed for basis point increases. If the total from the employees on the team matches or exceeds 100 basis points, the supervisor will qualify for the $2,000 bonus, provided the other requirements are fulfilled. These requirements are described below.

4. Time Restrictions

• Each Mentoring round should have a definitive time period, for example two months. An adequate period of time is required for the supervisor to motivate the mentored employees and implement the mentored employees' ideas. Also, a definite ending time should be established in order to determine the success of the program and the accrual of basis points for supervisory bonuses.

• A period of time should be established to make certain that the productivity increases attained by the mentored employees are stable and will not dissipate after the Mentoring round has ended. At least a month should be set aside as an appropriate period of time for productivity level maintenance.

5. Requirements for $2,000 Bonus

• A supervisor must attain at least 100 basis points from the Mentored team.

• The productivity levels that created the 100 basis points must be maintained for at least one month after the Mentoring round ends.

• The Operating Manager must remove the FTE from the workforce by one of the following methods:

– Attrition — the avoidance of hiring a new employee when one leaves the company.

– Free Time — the Operating Manager must confirm that 40 hours a week in additional Free Time was produced as a result of the supervisor's Mentoring efforts.

– Permanent Layoff — if attrition or increased Free Time does not produce an FTE reduction, then the FTE must be attained by layoff

6. Quality Qualifier

• As with gainshares, the mentored employees must be above the quality standards in order for the basis points to count toward the supervisor's bonus.

7. Round Two

• At the discretion of the Operating Manager, a second mentoring round can be established after the completion of the first Mentoring round. Many Distribution Centers discover they are able to spin off several FTEs, although only a handful of their supervisors hit the $2,000 bonus. For example, if the facility has 10 supervisors who all attain only 50 bonus points each, the facility as a whole will have 500 basis points, and the opportunity to spin off 5 FTEs.

• Round two is run the same way as round one, and the supervisors pick a second team to mentor.

• Supervisors are allowed to keep their same team from round one. This team of Mentored employees will require minimal maintenance, perhaps only a minute a day for each employee. This will allow the supervisor time to devote to the Mentoring efforts required by the second team.

• Basis point calculations are determined from the productivity levels of each team's employees. The round one employees are benchmarked from when they started round one until the end of round two. The round two employees are benchmarked from the beginning of round two. For example, if a supervisor has 60 basis points from the round one employees and 40 basis points from the round two employees, then the supervisor has 100 total basis points and can qualify for the $2,000 bonus, provided the other requirements are met (as discussed in section 5).

Brainstorming Techniques

The procedure of brainstorming is fairly simple. However, there are a few twists and secrets that can make all the difference in your degree of success with this powerful tool.

First let's go over the basics:

• Select your group of brainstormers. Try to keep the group below 10, as smaller groups are more conducive to bubbling up ideas.

• Give the group your problem to solve at least a day or two ahead of the brainstorming session so their subconscious minds have a chance to churn over the problem. Ideally, the problem to solve should be one of the audacious goals, such as "How Do We Increase Productivity 30%?"

• Choose a conference room where you can have a private meeting, and have a flip chart or white board ready.

• Select a moderator who can keep the session rolling, and someone to record all the ideas.

• Set the rules: There are no incorrect or ridiculous ideas or answers. Quantity counts in this group, not quality. No one is to ridicule or demean anyone's idea. In fact, announce that you encourage wild or even absurd ideas. After all, Albert Einstein once said, "If at first the idea is not absurd, then there is no hope for it."

• Start with a warm-up session. Our favorite warm-up is to provide the group a joke from a joke book, then instruct them to change the topic or components of the joke as you go round robin with the brainstorming participants. We've found this joke topic always breaks the ice and gets everyone participating.

• When you begin your real topic (such as, "What do we need to do to accomplish a 30% increase in productivity?") continue going round-robin around the room. This way everyone knows they'll both have a chance to participate and be expected to say something when their turn arrives. Choose a topic magnanimous enough to be worthy of everyone's time and effort. The bigger the stretch, the better.

• When the brainstorming session stalls, send the group on a short ten-minute break. We found breaks are a good way for their subconscious minds to work out various problems and solutions.

• When the group returns, start a normal brainstorming session again; when the group runs out of steam again, see if they can build on the ideas already listed. When the group stalls again, repeat the 10-minute break.

• This time when the group returns, take the list of ideas created in the prior sessions and ask the group to invert them. Sometimes it's quite fruitful to examine the opposite of the prior ideas, and this is a good way to come across a great idea.

• Close the session when the idea-inversion technique is completed, or try one more regular session.

Now, let's talk about the main pitfall to brainstorming. Why do some managers create winning ideas with the brainstorming technique, while others come away with only a few mediocre suggestions? The answer is simple — repetition. The average manager gives up on brainstorming when the ideas dry up in the first session.

But audacious managers, like any great leader of history, stay completely focused on the ultimate objective. Audacious managers know the human mind will continue working away at solving problems long after the brainstorming session ends, even when the participants are engaged in entirely unrelated activities. This explains why innovative ideas pop into mind at the oddest times, like when you are taking a shower or shaving. The same subconscious process causes some people to bolt upright in bed to exclaim, "Eureka!" when an idea jumps into a dream.

So the audacious manager or brainstorming leader needs to tap into this source of creativity by conducting repeated sessions, every one to two weeks, until the goal has been attained by the participants creating brainstorming ideas. It's important, though, to keep the sessions fresh. Below are suggestions for spicing up the repeating brainstorming sessions:

• Vary the site. Go outdoors for a brainstorming session. Go to a restaurant or boat or park or resort. Some of the most productive sessions occur in taverns. We even heard of a successful session at a bowling alley, the ideas called for between frames!

• Vary the leader. Rotate the session leadership or bring in different leaders from other areas of the company.

• Hold a session — or a part of a session — during which only the most weird or wild idea can be stated by the participants.

• Conduct a "lightning round" where each participant must state an idea as you go round-robin every 10 seconds per participant.

The point we're trying to stress here is to be incessant. We assure you if you stay focused on the final objective over a period of many weeks, and don't give up when the generation of ideas hits a period of drought, you will eventually produce more than enough ideas to attain your audacious goal. The secret is to keep conducting various brainstorming sessions until you attain your goal.

Sample Corporate Sponsor Email For Mentoring

Below is an email sent out to supervisors by a corporate sponsor who was in the middle of implementing a mentoring program in his network. Feel free to use any of this text to frame your own communications. You can see that the email was based on some of our writings.

To all supervisors:

As we discussed on the conference call last Thursday, I wanted to underline the three fundamentals of what we're all trying to achieve in our Mentoring Program.

Basically the math is simple — if a DC has 100 employees, and we raise all their productivity 10%, that's a potential of 10 FTEs we can remove without any difference at all in our ability to get the daily production done.

Let's take a look at the three ways our supervisory staffs can make this vision come to reality:

Touch base with your mentored employees daily

Each mentored employee has a different set of attention needs. In the beginning of the mentoring effort, an employee might require 15 to 20 minutes a day, or even longer. A month into mentoring, the same employee might only require a minute or two each day. But the most important thing to remember is that every mentored employee needs a "touch" each and every day from the supervisor to re-enforce the mentoring effort. Many times just a few seconds a day is all it takes to keep the mentored employee forging ahead.

Keep the 40% goal before their eyes

We all have to remember — both mentors and mentored employees — and have it re-enforced daily, that the stretch goal is to achieve a 40% increase in productivity, or the corresponding amount of Free Time. This is why employees sign up for the program, although they may not have realized at the beginning that it meant a 40% increase in productivity. All the same, it's up to us to manage them toward this achievement.

Indeed, if you buy into the Pete the Pipe Guy theory that an employee doesn't have to be an Olympic athlete to make $20 an hour, then you understand the importance of daily reinforcement. Because the fact remains that the best way to make $20 an hour is to zone in on the work and waste absolutely no time during the day.

It would be nice — and pretty darn easy — if we could simply instruct all the mentored employees to waste no time during the day. Unfortunately, it's not that simple. Instead employees must come to this realization themselves. In the end, this is why Mentoring is so effective and is bearing fruit for us: It's a good way to help employees come to the conclusion to waste no time, and — with the use of Gainsharing — reward them for buying into these concepts.

Manage the Seven Stages

Let's face it, it wasn't very difficult to get employees to sign up for Mentoring in order to get a $2-an-hour raise. The hard part quickly began, though, when they understood the $2 raise required a 40% increase in productivity. Instantly, it produced in them a Stage One reaction:

Denial

Employee: "40! I don't think I'll ever be able to do 40!"

Possible supervisory response: "Well now, just wait a minute, nobody said you have to hit 40% tomorrow. Let's both you and I keep touching base and see if we can come up with ways for you to get there eventually. There are probably a hundred little things we can do to pick up a percent or two."

During following weeks, mentoring supervisors have seen all the other six stages.

Bargaining

Employee: "I'll never be able to hit that 40% unless the Company does _____, or fixes _____, or straightens out _____."

Possible supervisory response: "We're working on it, but I don't know if we're going to get it done in the immediate future. On the other hand, this DC has a lot of employees already at 40%. Let's concentrate on those things you and I can directly control in the meantime and see if we can get you headed toward that $2."

Disbelief

Employee: "I don't believe those stories about Pete the Pipe Guy — he's got to be cheating or using a magic pencil."

Possible supervisory response: "Yeah, a 220% gainshare seems out of this world, but I don't think he was cheating. His manager reported that Pete hit his numbers because he's fanatical about wasting no time at all during the day — not a single, solitary second. He's totally focused on his goal of hitting the next gainshare level."

Anger

Employee: "Stop bugging me each day! Take me off this stupid program!"

Possible supervisory response: "Don't worry. If you want to get out, I'll sign you off the program. But why not take a couple days and think it over. I'll check back with you at the end of the week."

Guilt and/or Depression

Employee: "I just can't do it. I guess I'm not as good as those other workers."

Possible supervisory response: "Hey, don't be so hard on yourself. All you have to do is your own personal best, and don't worry about those other employees. Let's just control what you and I can control each day — and what we control is us both doing our own best each day. How about if we just take it a little bit at a time, and see what happens?"

Throughout any of the above stages, a running theme is for the mentored employee to come to the conclusion that one of the big secrets of attaining the 40% goal is to waste no time during the day. This battle will be won in minutes gained each day, and not by an abrupt leap up to the 40% level. Our supervisory efforts must be focused on ways to keep our mentored employees thinking about the 40% goal and the easiest ways to reach it.

Maybe the trick is to understand that we all — yes, every one of us — go through our own Seven Stages. Each employee has their own time frame, and travels their own course through the Seven Stages. Some employees even skip stages. We must understand that our role is to manage them, and ourselves, through all the stages, and never allow an employee to get hung up on any one stage but Acceptance. This will bring us all success.

As I mentioned during the conference call, Carl Jung once said, "We cannot change anything until we accept it." Our role is to help our mentored employees accept the 40% goal as something they can eventually achieve as long as they doggedly pursue it.

Characteristics of an Effective Corporate Sponsor

• The corporate sponsor should be knowledgeable of the blue-collar workforce and empathetic with their problems and challenges. Ideally, the corporate sponsor is an upper manager or executive who started in the blue-collar ranks and worked his or her way up in the company.

• The corporate sponsor should have good leadership skills and the respect of the facility managers.

• It's important that the facility managers report to the corporate sponsor, either directly or by a dotted line. As such, the sponsor should be a current or former facility manager. If a current facility manager, a promotion should occur to the position of corporate sponsor. It's better this person be from an operating position rather than Human Resources. Other than the importance of the reporting relationship, it's critical that the corporate sponsor be able to spot the "Project Junkies."

• The corporate sponsor needs to be a zealot for Simplified Gainsharing, and a person with good speaking skills. He or she must be familiar, and keenly believe in, the Simplified Gainsharing material. The corporate sponsor must also be able to incessantly drive a program on a corporate level.

• The corporate sponsor should be a skillful trainer, one able to relate to all levels of the organization — from blue-collar to executive. He or she also needs to be a good coach, one cognizant of the "Seven Stages of Managerial Death."

• The corporate sponsor needs good institutional knowledge of the company. He or she needs to understand the financial math of Simplified Gainsharing and be meticulous about tracking each facilities' performance on a monthly basis.

• The corporate sponsor needs to empathize with the "Free Money Police" and take pains to periodically demonstrate the substantial financial synergies of Simplified Gainsharing, making the financial guardians of the company comfortable with the bonus payouts.

• The corporate sponsor should be a person who is a good talent scout, someone who can identify which supervisors in the facilities are skillful with the Simplified Gainsharing rollout. This trait will come in handy during the mentoring stages.

• The corporate sponsor should be willing to travel. A network rollout will require regular visits to all facilities.

Poetry of Resurrection

One of the authors of the tome currently resting in your hands is a fairly regularly published poet, with over 1,600 publications to date. Pretty prolific, but he would be the first to state he is the most minor of minor poets. A few words might be in order to ponder what — if any — impact this proclivity for poetry had on *Warehouse Productivity* and the idea of workforce resurrection.

First, there appears to be an interesting relationship between the ultra-subjective or profoundly intuitive field of poetry and the keenly mathematical matter of business. Not to mention the pursuit of poetry kept the author in the blue-collar ranks for a few years longer than his current business peers at the beginning of his career, 35 years ago.

One result might have been that poetry kept him closer to the blue-collar workforce than some other disciplines. Since only a handful of poets actually make a subsistent living from selling poetry, our poet coauthor was able to interact with the blue-collar workforce longer, before he himself began to be promoted upward into the managerial ranks. Not that this blue-collar discussion is akin to some anthropological study of unknown tribes — it isn't. Indeed, in many respects blue-collar folks are living more admirable lives than us corporate types.

Basically poets see what is evident to them but not always readily apparent to the general public; then they figure out the best words to describe what they have perceived in order to transmit it to everyone else. Perhaps some of these same dynamics occurred during the writing of this book. We mentioned in the Preface that the principles we were about to relate were not necessarily new or unique. Yet one wonders why such simple principles, which readily produce significant savings to any company, are not more widely in use. Perhaps all these principles needed to be brought together in one place; perhaps they needed to be organized into a simplified system that, if followed closely, will work each and every time it's implemented in a facility.

One thing that can be said for the logistics industry — it's enamored with numbers. Nearly everything we do, and nearly every plan we create, is profoundly based on mathematics. Yet much of what we discussed in this book is predicated more on human nature and people simply doing what's in their best interests. Maybe it needed a poet to help put the system together in a manner that best focuses on how to harness human nature. For while all these principles are not unique, what is indeed unique about *Warehouse Productivity* is the impetus for profit that is created by utilizing a system that mimics the free enterprise system for the blue-collar workers.

At any rate, we're quite honored that you made it to the very end of this book, and are grateful you've taken the time to consider our thoughts and principles. We hope you will experience as much success with these ideas as we've experienced.

Lastly, if you're ever in the mood for reading a little poetry, we invite you to take a look at www.wardkelley.com. Our poet coauthor writes his poetry under the pen name of Ward Kelley, and would be quite happy if you stopped by.